How You Can Get a Better Job

There is always work, and tools to work withal,
for those who will.

JAMES RUSSELL LOWELL

How YOU Can Get a Better Job

BY

WILLARD K. LASHER

Vice President and
Director of Extension Division
American Technical Society

Past Divisional Chairman of Vocational Guidance
and Placement for Illinois-Eastern Iowa
District of Kiwanis International

AND

EDWARD A. RICHARDS, Ph.D.

Formerly Associate Director of University Extension
Columbia University

———

AMERICAN TECHNICAL SOCIETY
CHICAGO, U.S.A.

1952

 2

PRINTED IN THE U. S. A.

Foreword

THIS BOOK IS FOR MEN AND WOMEN who are seeking
employment, or for those who are determined to leave
the jobs they are doing, not by quitting, but by earning a promotion.

Promotion comes to those who increase their worth;
seldom to others.

Increasing one's worth, however, is something more
than acquiring additional skill and knowledge. To be
sure, it is made up largely from these two important
assets, but to them we must add others equally important—character, tact, leadership, honesty, and courage.

The part you play in the great pattern of American
business will be determined in great measure by your
application of certain fundamental principles of thinking and acting. We hope to tell you in this book what
these fundamentals are in order that you may deserve
and win advancement.

Notice the words "deserve" and "win." On every
street corner you'll find someone ready to tell you that
rewards in business do not go to those who deserve
them; that rewards come from pull, from "chiseling,"
from almost anything except ability, integrity, tact,
and earnest endeavor. Obviously, if you accept this
belief this book is of no use to you. Such a point of

view is not only cynical and disillusioning; it is fantastic and false.

It is true that in every community, in every large business, there are a few who hold their jobs, and perhaps are given promotion, because of influences that have nothing to do with their ability and ambition and character. It doesn't take very keen powers of observation, however, to see that such cases total a small number in comparison to the great army of people who make American business tick. As Mr. Kettering of General Motors says, "You can't have a man in an important job just because he is somebody's relative." The privates, the lieutenants, the generals in our industrial army hold their jobs and take on others— they get their medals and citations because they win them and deserve them.

Ability, hard work, tact, energy, and honesty are among the forces that, in Kipling's phrase, "show you the way to promotion and pay." You and I and millions of other Americans have only what we win—a fact so simple it is often forgotten. In any event, it is the foundation on which this book is built.

CONTENTS

PART I — THE HUMAN ELEMENT

PART II — SELF-MANAGEMENT

PART III — SELLING YOURSELF

PART IV — GETTING AHEAD

In all things success depends upon previous preparation.

CONFUCIUS 561–478 B.C.

PART I

The Human Element

Well-arranged time is the surest mark of a well-arranged mind.

OLD PHILOSOPHER 1940

Teamwork and Earning Power

THE SCENE—any American town. The time, between
seven and nine o'clock any week-day morning—the
rush hour. Some time before, folks in houses and
bungalows in the suburbs have begun to wake and
stir. In apartment houses, too, in tiny flats, in hotels,
men and women wake up, and stretch, and dress, and
get breakfast. Then they walk—if they're late they
probably run—to catch a street car or a bus or a
train. The morning tide of workers has begun to
flow. It's another day.

There are millions and millions of them—of us.
We wake each morning of every working day expect-
ing to spend most of our time and thought until we
get back home (and perhaps even afterward) on our
lifework. The word "lifework" isn't an idle one by
any means. It describes one of the three great areas
in which we all live. One of these areas is the community we live in, its society, its politics, its enter-
tainment, its demands upon us as citizens. The second
area is the area of our family, the most important
social group to which we belong. But family and community mean very little to us, and we mean very little
to them, if our lifework is left out of consideration.

1

In these three areas we squander or wisely invest our liberal allotment of time. By simple mathematics we find that there are 168 hours in every week. About 56 hours are, or should be, spent in sleep. We are awake 112 hours, and we spend between 40 and 50 hours either doing or thinking about our lifework—almost half, you see. The work we do and the associations we make during our working hours color our feelings, our ideas, and our attitude toward all other aspects of our lives. Feelings of pride, of accomplishment, of worth to our family and to our community are all deeply affected by the way we feel about our work, and by the way we do it. There is no doubt that men and women in business have a consuming interest in the work they do. They spend their best hours—the hours in which they are freshest—and their best years—the years in which their abilities are at the highest point on the curve—in making some definite contribution toward building and maintaining the towers of American business. Their ambitions, many of their strongest emotions, and many of their most delightful social experiences are bound up with the work which is their lifework.

These things are obvious enough, of course. What have they to do with our behavior? What's more, what can they possibly have to do with our earning power? The answer is simple. If it is true that we spend a great portion of our time—our most active years—in helping to conduct a business, it follows that what we do, both on and off the job, has a decided influence on our worth to an employer.

The title of this chapter might well be, "Tell me what you do and I'll tell you what you are." Frank analysis of your interests and pursuits, the things you do day by day and week by week, will tell you or any one more about the direction in which you are going than any amount of discussion of your ideas and ambitions could possibly tell. Interests inherent in a particular type of work are not separate, or wholly associated with one's business life. For example, a young man who is earnest in his desire to become an expert accountant will eagerly study a course designed to further his ambition. He will not find the economics of business a dull topic, as perhaps many do; rather, he will regard it as a topic of absorbing interest, and one vitally related to his personal life.

Do You Live on a Desert Island?

Alexander Selkirk was cast on a desert island; he was entirely alone, and according to the poem Alexander spouted:

> I am monarch of all I survey,
> My right there is none to dispute.

Every now and then we think how wonderful it would be to share Selkirk's experience and "get away from it all." No more cares, no worries, no pattern for living, *no other people.* Certainly this is one of the strangest of strange dreams. A day is all the solitude most of us can stand. Months and years of depending on ourselves alone? Not if we can help it!

People crowd around us on every side—family, friends, enemies, strangers, competitors. *We depend on every one of them. They are essential to us. Our lives have no meaning without them. And every one of our actions, no matter how apparently detached and isolated, influences our neighbor in some way.*

If you like to think you are independent, a real "lone wolf," just try it some time. You will find, perhaps, that like Mr. Selkirk you are "monarch of all you survey," but actually you are King of Nothing. You are a cipher, because there is nobody with you. You are not a "lone wolf" at all; you are a member of society (if you aren't grateful for the fact, you ought to be!). You are not one person alone, but one among many.

Let us consider for a moment the questions of time and individual rights. Almost half your waking hours are spent on the job working with other people. Your own task is tiny compared with the jobs of all your co-workers taken together. Your rights, your ambitions, your feelings do not merit consideration apart from theirs. They are human beings as well as you. You can't hope to get anywhere, or to get anything done except in relation to the whole organization of which you are a unit.

So—act accordingly. Don't *say* you are interested in other people, don't *claim* that you are considerate and cooperative. Prove it by what you do. Genuine understanding of and consideration for other members of your office or your department come before everything else. If you lack these qualities, and demonstrate your lack of them by your actions, well, you not only may fail of promotion when the time comes, you may be asked to leave; or you will become so unhappy and feel so ill-used that you will get out of your own accord.

Consideration for others—that is the thing that promotes cooperation, unity of purpose. Also, it is the basis of good manners. Also, it takes your mind off yourself and puts it where it belongs—on the job to be done and the means of doing it.

It Takes Knowledge Plus

Before the great explorer, Admiral Byrd, set out on the Antarctic Expedition in which he established Little America, he spent years in research. Reports and records of all previous expeditions as to weather, people, animals, ice floes, currents, and marine life, not only at the pole itself but all along the way, were carefully studied.

In addition to learning all he could about where he was going and what he could expect to encounter along the way, there was also the job of assembling a mountain of supplies and selecting a crew. The selection of the crew was of utmost importance to the expedition. He selected his men not only on the basis of their experience, knowledge, and physical fitness, but on their ability to get along with their fellow men.

Admiral Byrd knew that an expedition, like an athletic contest or a business endeavor, could fail miserably if the members participating did not recognize and adhere to the simple rules upon which almost any successful undertaking involving more than one person is based—TEAMWORK.

Teamwork Pays Dividends

Have you ever watched a professional or college football team? If you have, you have witnessed a fine example of teamwork. Each player has a position to cover—a certain job to do. He doesn't try to cover all the territory himself or make all the spectacular plays. He does the one job assigned to him, and the manner in which he does that job in a measure determines the success of the entire team.

Back in the days when Tom Harmon held the collegiate football spotlight, sports writers all over the country wrote column after column about his spectacular touchdowns. Each of these writers knew, however, that behind this brilliant player were ten other men working as a team to open holes in the opposing line to let Harmon through for one of his thrilling touchdown runs.

To be outstanding in its field a business organization must work in the same manner as did that great University of Michigan team back in the days of Tom Harmon.

Every job, big or small, is important to the success of a business organization, and when every individual is "on his toes" doing his best, and giving earnest cooperation to his fellow workers, that's teamwork.

Getting Along with Folks Ranked Next to Ability in Job

To illustrate the point further, an article by William F. McDermott, which appeared in the Chicago *Daily News,* July 31, 1940, is printed in part:

"If you emote easily you'd better stay out of business. But if you're a good-natured sort of person, who

gets along well with folks and is eager to make good, you've got every chance in the world to hold down an excellent job with a corporation. Adaptability is second only to ability to perform the task itself."

Such is the conclusion of Mrs. Jane H. Eastburn, for 17 years dean of women of the Standard Oil Company of Indiana and employment manager of its general offices in Chicago. In the latter capacity she has interviewed 60,000 men and women, young and old, looking for jobs. She will retire next month on a company annuity.

Requirements Change

"We used to hear a lot about 'soulless corporations,'" commented Mrs. Eastburn, "but that has largely passed. At one time efficiency was the sole objective. Business was supposed to be impersonal. If you could perform the mechanics of your job a little better than anyone else, that was all that was asked.

"Times have changed and the human element has become very important. The most desired employee is the one who can fit into the picture harmoniously and cheerfully.

"That's why emotional stability, cooperativeness, courtesy, dependability, and good nature are stressed so much by employment managers today. The person who is sulky, hypersensitive, inclined to fits of temper or jealousy, who resents constructive criticism, and is suspicious of fellow workers is under a severe handicap no matter how great the working efficiency. . . ."

Here are some questions you can ask yourself about

your behavior on the job. The answers will show you whether you are acting like a fit member of society, like a decent human being, or like a "lone wolf," a King of Nothing whatever. The questions follow:

Do I try to blame others for my own mistakes?

Do I take obvious pleasure in putting a fellow worker on the spot?

What do I say and *how* do I say it when I arrive in the morning?

Do I walk and carry myself as though I had some self-respect?

Do I try to get credit for the good work of others?

Is my own work done well within a reasonable time?

Do I spread malicious gossip? Or listen to it?

Do I learn something new every week about my job and matters related to it?

Do I show sympathetic interest in the fortunes and misfortunes of my fellow workers?

Do I willingly "pitch in" in emergencies?

Do I treat my place of business as if it were a place in which to get work done, or as if it were a lounging room?

Can I take a licking if I deserve it, and profit by it?

Can I stand up for myself in a temperate way if I feel I have been unjustly treated? Or do I hold a grudge and work it out in some underhanded way?

Am I willing to play my part in group activities, or do I shy away from them?

This is a long list. It could be longer, of course, and as you get interested in the subject, you can extend it yourself.

Good behavior is a mark of intelligence. It's just plain good old common sense to so conduct ourselves that those who work with us, or for us, like us and respect us. It is the people we work with who boost us up the ladder or pull us down. Yes, from every point of view, it is smart to behave in such a manner that we cannot be overlooked for promotions and salary increases.

You Are in the Spotlight

It's a good thing to remember that on a job you are like an actor taking part in a play. You didn't build the plot yourself, or select the rest of the cast, or arrange for hiring the theater, or choose the scenery and lighting. You have a part—only a part. And there you are, up front on the stage, with the spotlight focused on you.

The people playing with you depend upon you to remember your lines. They depend upon you for support. You take your cues from them and they take theirs from you. If you don't show up on time, if you fumble your lines, if you are careless or don't act your part, you spoil the production—and they'll have to call in a substitute to perform your part.

The people "out front" are looking at you, too—every act, every word and gesture. But you don't mind that. You forget they are there. You are one of a company of players putting on the show. You "throw" yourself into your part. You get a tremendous "kick" out of it—the show is a great success. It makes money for the producer. And if your performance pleases everybody, the chances are you'll get a chance to play a bigger role later on—you win a promotion.

Promotion comes to those who increase their worth—seldom to others. To increase your worth you must do more than increase your knowledge. You must also observe or put into practice those rules that make you the kind of person with whom other people like to work.

Shop Talk

IN SHOP WORK a man's ability or knack for doing the work, or his lack of it, shows up in a hurry. There's something pretty sharp and clear about machine or tool work of any kind. Nowhere does lack of skill or aptitude show up more plainly. On construction jobs, in wood-working plants, machine shops, and on metal work of all kinds, the machines and the materials themselves will show up very quickly a fellow's strong and weak points.

If you have survived for a considerable length of time in such a place, if the materials and tools haven't licked you, then you can be pretty sure that you are on the right track as far as mechanical skill is concerned. What else is there? A great deal, as you know. Broadly speaking, there is production, the drafting room, engineering (including research), and sales. Your superiors probably have their own ideas as to whether you are good material for any of these lines. But leaving them out of the discussion, I think it's pretty largely up to you to find out which is best for you. Maybe not any. Your advancement may consist of one of the greatest forms of progress—that of continuously perfecting your skill as a craftsman. If that is so, *don't be ashamed of it.* For the truly skillful craftsman who can make steel and wood and wire seem to live and breathe is among the greatest of living beings. If that's your kind of career, take it, and thank God for your skill, because you belong to a select company.

On the other hand, perhaps you are an exceptionally good machinist, but the thing that really stirs your blood is the push and drive of production work. You like to have a picture of *all* the wheels going around together according to plan. You think you've got the makings of a production man—a shop executive, a foreman, supervisor, or superintendent.

Analyze Yourself

There are several ways in which you can check on this ability in yourself to see whether you really possess it, or whether you just fancy that you do.

First of all, when you are doing your job, do you do it with a sense of partnership in all the other work going on around you? Or do you think of your work as just an isolated item off in a corner somewhere? In other words, have you got any talent—or any real desire—to see the operation as a whole?

Can you find anything in your job, or in the way that you do it, that slows down production?

Have you any feeling of pride in the total output of your shop or department?

How Is Your Timing?

And what about time with respect to production? Do you coordinate your activities? Do you like to work out long or short schedules and then try to meet them? This question might be put in a way familiar to all who like sports: How's your timing? Your sense of rhythm?

Again, take your activities when you are away from the shop. Do you ever try to organize and coordinate the work or the play activities of your friends and neighbors?

In general, do people go along with your ideas easily, or do you meet a lot of resistance?

If you do not like to plan and organize, if people will not work cheerfully with you and for you, if you are "off" in your timing, you will need to have exceptional skill to win promotion to the job of foreman, superintendent, or production manager.

This does not mean, however, that you must give up hope of reaching an executive position. It may be that along with your mechanical skill, you have the rare ability to *visualize*. If you do, and if you turn naturally to books and discussions on engineering problems, your road ahead lies through drafting, design, and engineering. Or maybe you have just that unusual blend of technical information and sales sense that will eventually put you in the front line on the sales force.

Mr. William S. Knudsen of General Motors (a member of the National Defense Council during World War II) indicates briefly the natural disposition of workers in an industrial organization, in accordance with their abilities. His statement follows:

People Divide Themselves According to Their Ability into Three Groups

"I call these three groups the searchers, the teachers and the doers. Industry needs all three of these groups."

We Need Searchers

"We need searchers to look forward into what we are going to do. We need these searchers to record what has been done and to try to glean from that those things that are good."

We Need Teachers

"We need the teachers because the teacher is really the head of our distribution process in the United States. A good salesman is nothing but a good teacher. We certainly can't deny the fact that with all our capacity to produce, our products wouldn't be worth anything unless we could find somebody to distribute them."

We Need Doers

"Now when we come to the doers, there is no better experience for a young man than to take something apart and put it together again, because after he has done something with his hands, he can do it in his mind. When he can do it in his mind he is an engineer."

Keen application to your job, keen realization of how it fits into the general picture, and *study of your own habits outside the job,* will do two things:

First, such procedure will give you a pretty good idea of the road you should follow.

Second, it will offer clear proof to those watching you that you are not only distinctly worth *watching*, but worth *pushing*.

It would be to good purpose if a surgical instrument could be devised that would cut out a certain little fungus that grows in the brain of many. This growth is nourished by the falseness of be-liefs such as, "There's no opportunity any more," or "Nobody cares whether my work is good or not," and so on, far, far into the night—and perhaps half the next morning, too. Don't let us deceive ourselves. Dissatisfied, self-styled "ambitious" people are easy to find. People whose ambitions are founded on consciousness of their abilities, on their capacity for hard work and their willingness to cooperate, are worth their weight in dollar bills—and the combination isn't easy to find. Ask any personnel manager. Ask anyone who is in the market for such people. They'll tell you. Loyalty here, brains there, energy over yonder, worlds of cheap "push" and wild personal claims—but not very often real ambition and the other qualities *all in the same package*. And that desired combination, of course, is the mark to shoot at. Don't worry about not being noticed. You won't have to. You will be noticed in spite of everything. For the people who aim at high marks are always only a few compared to the great mass of their fellows.

Shops differ greatly, of course, in the materials manufactured and in the skills they require in the men they employ, but certain matters are always important no matter what kind of shop you work in. Pay close attention to the following points:

Take Every Opportunity To Learn

Many shops give training courses during hours or after hours. Show an interest in these, and if you can possibly do so, attend them. It may be that you will be required to attend; in this case, don't resent the requirement but welcome the chance. Let your superintendent know that you want to increase your knowledge and skill, and ask his advice about how to do it. He may be able to open your eyes to ways of doing things that had never occurred to you.

You will be taught from the minute you step inside the shop. In all probability you will receive on starting a fairly good-sized book or pamphlet containing all the general shop rules and policies. In addition, the foreman or superintendent will have a great deal to say about your job and everything relating to it. In addition, you may find signs and instruction sheets posted around the plant. Don't pass up any of these sources of information. As you read or listen, be sure that you understand, and be sure to ask as many questions as you need to get an entirely clear picture of what is expected of you.

This warning is perhaps all the more necessary if you are an old hand, comparatively speaking, and have had quite a bit of experience at the same general type of work. Perhaps you were hired mainly on account of such experience. But it isn't safe for you to assume that this gives you the information you need on how this particular shop is run. The machines, the routines, the regulations, probably all will be a little different. So keep your eyes and ears open until you feel at home in your new surroundings. It may be hard for an "old dog" to learn new tricks, but he must make the effort; and of course the beginner, feeling his way in a new field, must keep on his toes.

Alertness and Attention

There are special reasons for these qualities in shop work. Lack of them may cause misunderstandings of orders and specifications, inefficiency in routines, injury to yourself, or damage to costly machines and materials. Some of these points we want to mention later in relation to safety on the job, but they are so closely connected with alertness and attention that they also deserve mention here.

Naturally, all mistakes are troublesome and in some

degree avoidable, but there is much difference in the consequences of errors of various kinds. If you make a mistake in multiplication on a piece of scrap paper, you can soon find it and correct it. No great harm is done; you merely didn't get the right answer when you should have. But suppose you make a mistake in the number, diameter, or location and arrangement of holes drilled in a costly steel plate! Such mistakes are obviously expensive—and inexcusable. Shop errors are almost immediately estimated in terms of destruction of property and injury to workers. It is strictly up to the worker himself to keep sharp and alert in order to do his part toward preventing waste and actual danger.

Learn to Read and Follow Printed Instructions

Good eyesight and concentration are the requirements here. Assuming that your instructions are correct, be sure first of all that you actually *see all* of what is before you, whether it's a printed sheet of specifications or a blueprint. Perhaps a good deal of your work is eye work, but most of it calls for reading. If this is so, if you are not a practiced reader, take extra care to get in your mind all the material before your eyes. Then keep your mind strictly on all details of the job until it is done, and done right.

Be a Good Housekeeper

This means respecting the tools you work with, taking good care of them, and keeping them neatly arranged when not in use. If you are supposed to turn them in at a tool room, be sure to do it. Keep them off the floor so that nobody will stumble over them. And when you stop work, leave the place you have been working at in neat condition.

Avoid "Horse Play"

Rough-housing and practical jokes are all right in their place, but that place isn't the shop—particularly around machinery in motion. This is a necessary safety measure, aside from the fact that such foolery is obviously inefficient and a bother to other people on the staff.

Don't Waste Time or Materials

Your care in avoiding waste will have a great deal to do with your value on the job and with your chances of promotion. No man is thought to be good timber for greater responsibility if he is careless about duties he already has.

The "Why" of Safety in the Shop

Some shop jobs are more hazardous than others, but in all shop work, and on construction jobs, there are greater hazards to be faced than any encountered in office work. The cost of accidents to individuals and to industry as a whole is an appalling thing—almost impossible to realize. For this reason, everyone from the company president down to the youngest apprentice has today become acutely conscious of the need for cutting down the staggering bills submitted and paid every year for industrial accidents. These bills, of course, are not summarized in terms of money alone, but also in terms of discomfort, pain, and crippled bodies.

Here are some figures on machine shop accidents occurring in the state of Ohio in a single year.

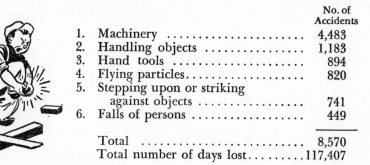

		No. of Accidents
1.	Machinery	4,483
2.	Handling objects	1,183
3.	Hand tools	894
4.	Flying particles	820
5.	Stepping upon or striking against objects	741
6.	Falls of persons	449
	Total	8,570
	Total number of days lost	117,407

According to arithmetic, this means over 300 calendar years lost by accidents to machine shop workers alone in *one* state, in *one* year. It doesn't seem possible—but there are the figures. Mr. Harry L. Sain of the Ohio Industrial Commission, who presents them, has some further things to say on the subject:

"The six causes [of accidents] previously mentioned are closely related to other causes, namely, faulty environment and faulty human behavior. These two causes can be further subdivided into mechanical and personal causes, such as:

a) Improper guarding.
b) Defective substances and equipment.
c) Hazardous arrangement of machinery, tools and equipment.
d) Improper and poor illumination.
e) Improper clothing or apparel.
f) Improper heating and ventilation.
g) Physical or mental defect.

23

h) Lack of knowledge or skill.
i) Wrong attitude.
j) Improper selection, direction and training
   of workers."

Notice the *personal* causes of accidents: "Improper clothing," "physical or mental defect," "lack of knowledge or skill," and "wrong attitude." Notice, too, that these things are closely related to the points we brought out earlier.

Ragged clothing, or loose, flapping clothing, is as unsafe as it is unsightly.

If you aren't properly "tuned up" physically and mentally, not only do you work inefficiently, but you lack the control necessary to protect yourself and guard against injury.

If you try to do jobs that you only pretend to understand, you are likely not only to spoil your work but hurt yourself seriously.

If you have the "wrong attitude," you are working against your own progress. For example, if you act as though you had nothing more to learn, if you think and say that safety devices are for softies, not for real "he-men" like you, if you refuse to follow suggestions and rules laid down on the basis of experience for your guidance and protection, you may have to learn a bitter lesson later on. On the other hand, one of the best ways to show your sense of good workmanship and efficiency is to cooperate on safety rules. They are designed for your personal safety, yes. But they are also designed for the sake of the company and are intended to prevent the waste in time and money which accidents always bring to the management. This cooperative attitude on safety will probably color all

24

your work in the shop. It will not only serve to protect you from injury, but it will show that you have good sense as well as mechanical skill, and are eager to use both for the good of the organization.

Four Short Rules for Increasing Your Pay Check

1. Do what you are doing the very best you know how.
2. Learn something new about your chosen field every day.
3. Make everybody you work and associate with like and respect you.
4. Keep alert—mentally and physically.

ONE SUMMER MORNING about 100 years ago, a young man climbed weather-beaten stairs to the loft of a long wooden building on a side street in Williamsport, New York. It was a pleasant place he stepped into— well lighted, with piles of seasoned boards, beautifully planed, and the clean fragrance of sawdust and shavings.

An old man with rounded shoulders, a bald head, and long gray whiskers looked up from his bench and growled a "Good morning" through his beard. He was old Lafe Brown, master carpenter and cabinetmaker.

"Good morning, sir," the young man replied, and in answer to the old gentleman's look of inquiry he went on, "Maybe you remember that ladder-back chair you made for my mother."

"Certainly I do." The old worker laid down his plane and rubbed his palm over the shining expanse of maple he had been working on. "Let's see now. That was 14, no, 15 years ago come Christmas. Your pa wanted it as a present, I recall."

"Yes, sir, that's right. How you do remember things! Well, I wish you'd make one exactly like it

26

for me—for Mary—you know we're going to be married next month."

"Yep, so I heard, so I heard— Hm-m. A month ain't much time, but let's see, I've got the stock all right—just the thing in fact. See that?" Lafe walked over to a pile and pulled up one end of a hickory plank. "Yep, that'll be just the thing. Hm-m. Yep. I'll have the chair for you, son." He smiled and rested his hand on his customer's shoulder. "It'll cost ye $15.00. Wives comes expensive, don't they? You come in on— let's see now—come in on the 12th and here it'll be, all ready for her to set down in."

That's all, except that the bridegroom *did* go back on the date specified, and the chair *was* ready and he *did* pay cash for it. Then he took it home and gave it to his wife and she sat in it with comfort whenever she wanted to for many years.

That Was Business 100 Years Ago

That was business. And very fine business, too. And nobody touched a pen or a pencil to a piece of paper while getting it done. The buyer went to the

27

maker, who was also the seller. They talked and agreed. The customer carried the finished article home. It was a good chair, and the buyer and his wife admired it. *No office work involved.* In other words:

No designing. (That had been done years before.)

No drawing. (Old Lafe had that in his head.)

No cost figuring. (That was in his head, too.)

No one to consult. (Old Lafe consulted with himself.)

No sales problem. (The customer came to buy.)

No advertising. (The old man had been doing business there for 50 years. Everybody knew him.)

No credit problem. (Old Lafe knew the bridegroom was worth the $15.00.)

No transportation worries. (The customer carried the goods home over his shoulder.)

No adjustment troubles or complaints. (The chair was the best of its kind, and still is usable although a century has gone by since Old Lafe first put it together.)

Such man-to-man, face-to-face business is still done, but it's the exception rather than the rule. The chair maker in Grand Rapids can't possibly sell all his chairs in his home town. And probably he will not know more than one or two of the people who purchase his product. He sells to wholesalers and retail dealers in San Diego, and New Orleans, and Portland, Maine. As a general thing they don't find him; he has to find them. They aren't known to him personally; they are no more than commercial units, "accounts," which enable him to continue turning out chairs. So he has to set up special machinery to sell, to advertise, to establish credit ratings, to bill, to collect money, to ship goods over great distances safely, and so on. The many things that old Lafe Brown was not required to do, the large-scale manufacturer must do if he is to survive.

Then again, our Grand Rapids man finds his customers more numerous and far more varied in their tastes and their ideas of fashion than was Lafe's clientele. Every year he tries out new designs, and variations of old ones—he experiments in woods, in design, in upholstery materials—all in the hope that more chairs, or at least as many, can be sold at a greater margin of profit than heretofore.

He Cannot Do It Alone

He cannot do it alone. Therefore he has quite a large staff of helpers—designers, salesmen, accountants, shippers, typists, correspondents. Sometimes he groans when he looks at the salary overhead, but he knows he might just as well be resigned. Many people, of widely differing tastes, living hundreds of thousands of miles distant, must be induced to buy his goods and must get them once they are bought. *He can't*

do it alone. No one department of his office can do it alone. A business organization is a composite force, a unified whole, each part working in harmony with all the other parts.

This is why so many people are "in business." The essential process is just the same now as it was when Lafe Brown made and sold the hickory chair. But the *steps* in the process have multiplied to the point where it is impossible for one man to handle them alone. More customers—more competition—greater distances —more fashion designing—more division of function such as manufacturer, dealer, retailer—equals more advertising, more shop workers, more typists, more salesmen—more helpers of every sort. That's the equation of modern business. That's the kind of arithmetic that puts furniture in our homes, food on our tables, clothes on our backs, and automobiles in our garages.

You Are Vitally Important

Turning for a moment to you, if you're working in an office, perhaps you think that you aren't essential to your organization. Perhaps *you* aren't. But your job, your function, *is* important if the organization is well put together. If you think your function is *not* important—well, you are probably the only person in the company who holds such an opinion.

We must stop here to check over some points that make a lot of difference in the kind of impression you make by your office habits. These things are "small but mighty." Of themselves they may not win you promotion, but promotion is practically out of the question unless you can make a high score on these points.

At the head of the list stands *promptness*. Why should we mention it? Simply because so many otherwise worthy people are not prompt by habit. Perhaps it is the fault of their training. Perhaps they were not taught to be on time when they were children. In any case, they must learn it later if not sooner if they expect to get ahead in business. Well—why? What difference do a few minutes make one way or the other? The time can be made up, they are perfectly willing to do so, etc. True, but irrelevant.

Take the Case of Tom Sidney

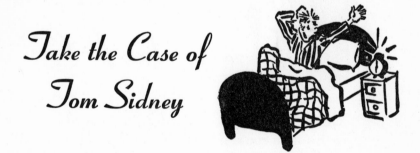

Take the case of Tom Sidney. He was a good man at his job, but he just couldn't get to the office on time in the morning, or come back from lunch at noon on time. He was always from five to fifteen minutes late.

When the matter was called to his attention he plainly showed his resentment, made a feeble effort for a few days to be on time, then drifted back to his old bad habits again. One day, when notified to be on time or leave, he put up this sort of an argument in his defense:

I don't see why so much fuss is made over the few minutes I'm late now and then. You admit I do my job well and you know I'm willing to work overtime whenever the work is heavy, so why can't I come in late now and then? Of course if it means my job I'll mend my ways.

Tom mended his ways, not because he wished to, but because he had to. Later, when he was being considered for the job of office manager, he was ruled out because of his lack of understanding of the basic reason for promptness in a business office.

You Sell Your Time for Cash

Office salaries represent a definite item of cost. In fact this item could almost go on the purchase ledger. The firm you work for buys your time by the hour and pays for it by the week or month. If you are hired to work, say forty hours a week, and if you are late in getting to the office in the morning or in returning to your desk after lunch, you are guilty of giving your firm "short weight." Any firm that continually accepts less than it pays for is operating on an unsound basis. That's point number one.

Point number two is even more important. Every office, large or small, must establish rules and regulations. If one person is allowed to break the rules, it naturally follows that others will expect to do so. This of course results in the general breakdown of office morale, a condition which can easily affect the working routine to a point where it will be the direct cause of serious loss of business. No man or woman can expect to be given a position of authority if he or she cannot understand and appreciate the necessity for office regulations and wholeheartedly abide by them. Rules tend to make an office run like a well-oiled piece of machinery. Tom Sidney could not or would not understand this; that is why he is still working at the same old job.

Be There When the Game Starts

You have to acquire the point of view that the business game can't be well played, with a good winning spirit, unless all the members of the team are on hand to start the first inning. Just imagine what would happen at a major league ball field if the manager of the team found at the last minute that his third baseman or the right-fielder he had counted on for his team's line-up wasn't on hand. Oh, he has utility men, sure. The game can go on—but not as he had planned. There will be delay, irritation, and later on some alibis and ill-feeling. No. The fact is if you've got a position to play you'd better get in there and play it from the time the game is called. Leave the excuses for someone else to make.

If promptness is the first common virtue and necessity in the successful operation of an office, then *accuracy* is second. We are not talking now about errors in judgment, but about errors in detail. They arise from much the same state of mind that produces tardiness, that is, from some kind of hidden desire *not* to do the job well. Psychologists tell us that no one is habitually late for appointments unless he secretly *wishes* to be late. For the same underlying reason, no one habitually makes errors unless secretly he is holding back from doing the task at hand. His mind wanders, and his eye and his fingers follow.

 Accuracy means a lot when promotions are being considered. There was the time that Frank Boynton was going to be given a better job in a larger office. He almost got it. And then somebody remembered that Frank was always making little mistakes. He would never recheck his work. *Somebody else* had to get it right, not Frank. And when mistakes were called to his attention, there was always a disagreeable flare-up. Promotion? No. *Too risky.*

With respect to accuracy, it is assumed that you are

in the physical condition necessary to efficient performance of your task. If you are doing eye work—
and most office workers do—then no amount of good
will on your part can compensate for poor eyesight.
If you handle a machine of some kind—and office
workers in general do at one time or another—
nothing can compensate for shaky nerves and tired
muscles—in short, fatigue. Get enough sleep and
rest. Have your eyes examined if necessary. If work-
conditions, such as poor light, are hampering you,
don't growl about it, but give your opinion to your
superior and ask his help. Ten to one you'll get it.

Errors Are the Bugbear of Business

Errors are the bugbear of business, they upset routine, increase the cost of doing business, lose good
customers and sometimes permanently wreck the career
of the person who made the mistake. Unfortunately,
news of a serious error generally gets right up to the
"head office," and along with it goes the name of the
person at fault. This puts the unfortunate individual
in the kind of "spotlight" that hinders promotion.

When given an important task to do, do it to the
very best of your ability and then check it before it
leaves your hands—in other words catch your own

errors. Keep out of the spotlight that balks promotion. Remember you can't expect an employer to give you greater responsibilities if you cannot handle accurately those you already have. Prove your ability and you will be prepared when opportunity comes.

Beware of Office Cliques

Unfortunately, few offices are free from small "pressure groups" that delight in embarrassing some person or persons outside the group by indulging in petty personal gossip.

These cliques are the most disrupting force in business offices. Generally, they form and operate during the lunch hour. Petty gossip or criticism about someone outside the group spreads, friction results, and, before it can be stopped, one group in the office is not talking to some other group or individual. Teamwork among these opposing factions is impossible; instead of cooperating, one group keeps constantly on the lookout for something to tell the boss about the other group. Often whole departments are at odds.

A keen, efficient office manager will smash such groups as fast as he discovers them—he knows how deadly they are. Stay out of such cliques. If you find yourself in such a group through no fault of your own, do not enter into the gossip. Stand up for the person or persons being gossiped about—refuse to be pulled into an office feud. No person working in an office can afford to make enemies of his fellow workers. It is just as important to be in good standing with the office boy as with the president, for if you expect promotion you must first prove that you can work with, as well as get cooperation from, others.

Guard Your Tongue

And guard your tongue against even mildly cutting remarks about your associates and their affairs. If people know you are eager to listen to gossip, you will make of yourself, not a desirable employee, but a yawning reservoir into which all gossip can be drained with the assurance that it will promptly be piped out again.

If you are in any doubt about the importance of a proper attitude in such matters, ask yourself these questions:

How would I feel if I knew that my boss was affected in all his attitudes and decisions by office gossip and office cliques? Would I respect him if I knew he spent an hour or so a day listening to and repeating idle tittle-tattle? The answer, of course, is an emphatic *No*. And the answer applies to you as well.

All this doesn't mean that you shouldn't have personal friends in the office. There, as elsewhere, you meet people with interests, or hobbies, or a background the same as, or similar to, your own. You like them, and they like you. You like to do things together after hours perhaps. Well, why not? Friendship is valued and respected under all circumstances. On the other hand, the qualities we have been talking about mean essentially an attitude opposed to friendship, and they are as dangerous as they are unpleasant. If you lend yourself to the petty traffic in personalities spread around the office, if you do any sniping at another person's ability or character, don't think that you will escape. Your turn will come. And since promotion depends to a greater extent than is usually realized on winning the esteem of one's peers, you can help to win that esteem by showing a fundamental decency in this matter of discussing personalities.

Office work is done through an orderly sequence of operations usually called routine. Lack of promptness, lack of accuracy, and indulgence in gossip of a personal nature tend to break or slow down this routine. Some other points to watch are the following:

Since your job is part of a sequence of routine operations, you probably have to receive instructions and orders, and pass them on. Probably you have to give some yourself. So, by all means, *keep the lines of communication open and clear*. Be sure you understand the instructions you get. If you do not, clear up all points before you proceed. This may mean careful checking of a written order. (Handwriting is not always readily legible.) Or it may mean a phone call, to straighten out instructions previously received by phone. In any case, be sure of your ground before you act. Once you do, don't be afraid to take full responsibility for what you have done. Maybe your judgment was good; maybe you made a mistake. But in either case, be the first to claim responsibility if any question arises. And, of course, if you are asked to take on extra duties, don't be afraid to say *yes*, even if they are new to you.

When you have occasion to give orders yourself, make sure that they are complete, clear, and accurate, and make sure, in a pleasant way, that the one who is getting the orders understands them. Clarity, completeness, and courtesy are the rules here.

Don't "Argufy"

Arguments are most likely to arise in connection with misunderstandings and errors pertaining to office routine. You are not often likely to encounter arguments over policy, but questions of personal responsibility and occasions when there is a difference of opinion about how a certain job should be done frequently arise.

Do not allow yourself to "argufy." Get two things clearly in mind. First, it's necessary to know all the important facts in a situation; second, it's necessary to *discuss* them in order to reach a solution. Never barge into a conversation with a statement like, "I know you're wrong there, because, etc., etc." The

39

argumentative style and tone will get you nowhere. Maybe you're right, but merely being right won't win you the liking and respect of your fellows. Benjamin Franklin was a great diplomat. He learned early that a positive, overbearing manner might win arguments but always lost good will. He learned to give his opinions by saying such things as, "I think," "Possibly this other way," "I believe," etc. The next time you find yourself in an argument, with all the black on one side and all the white on the other, see if you can't turn it into a *discussion* and reach a *solution*. It's not easy, but the ability to do this is worth pure gold in a business organization. For the purpose of business is not to conduct debating societies but to get work done in the pleasantest, most efficient way possible. Business is people, yes, but business is people organized into a little *special* society for a *special* purpose—to *do* business. Remember that and you can easily check up on your own office behavior, to determine whether it is helping or hindering your organization.

Personal Cleanliness

The manager of a Chicago unit of Sears, Roebuck and Co. retail stores has said that when interviewing applicants for the position of department manager the first things he looked at were their fingernails and shoes. Cleanliness of person is the first rule of good manners. Other people are sensitive to unpleasant odors and an unkempt appearance if you are not, and since the basis of good manners is consideration for the other fellow, make sure that skin, hair, nails, teeth, and breath are clean, and take care that perspiration odors are eliminated. Manufacturers of deodorants may sometimes overstate the danger of giving offense, but they have a lot of truth on their side, and one dares not relax caution in this regard. If you want people to like working with you, you must be careful to observe rules of personal hygiene.

Manners

A very important point in manners is your physical poise. At home in your own room you may sit or lie as you like, and you may gesture freely. When you are at business, you are in a house belonging to someone else, and you must use the same restraint you are careful to use when in the home of a person you know only fairly well. Furthermore, you are playing a part. You are acting for your company, not for yourself. At ten o'clock some morning you may feel like getting up to take a good stretch, or another time you may feel like whistling. You'd better check impulses of this kind. Such acts distract others and seem too unconventional for performance in public. Sagging or drooping posture indicates fatigue. Here is where you feel the advantage of getting a sufficient amount of sleep and exercise. For if your body is fit, you won't squirm into strange postures and you can maintain throughout the day the muscular and nervous control necessary to poise and good manners. To paraphrase an old saying, "Manners make the man." Remember it.

People who work with you and come in to do business with you see only what you show them; that is, they see how you behave. They are not interested in looking any deeper than that. As far as they are concerned, *your manners are you*.

There are thousands of laws on our statute books which name a penalty for failure to observe the injunctions they stipulate, from driving a car too fast to robbing a bank. On the other hand, while we live under the law, we don't regulate our daily conduct by law. The laws of good conduct are binding but are, for the most part, unwritten laws. To break them exacts not a legal penalty but a *social* one. And social penalties are very hard to bear. Every day people are barred from societies, social groups, jobs and promotions because their manners cause dislike and even distrust.

The expression "good manners" does not imply an affected or showy manner of speech or conduct. It doesn't mean bowing and scraping to your superiors. It doesn't necessarily mean observance of strict formality on all occasions. Fundamentally, good manners come from genuine consideration for the rights and privileges, the likes and dislikes, of others. To such practice should be added self-control in speech and conduct. If you behave in a too free and careless manner in the office, if you don't know how to carry yourself, if you talk too much about things that are of no concern to anyone but you, you are not only an inefficient employee but you are guilty of bad manners too. And your bad manners will trouble more people than your inefficiency, particularly if you contact the public in your work. Remember this:

Good manners grow from the root of kindness and consideration.

The Public Will Be Served

'WAY BACK in the 1890's, Hank Stebbins was running the general store in Littleton, Ohio. Hank didn't look like he amounted to much. You wouldn't pick him out of a crowd. In his store—where he spent almost all of his waking hours—he sort of melted into the background, just like one of his sacks of meal or a cluster of hoes and rakes leaning in the corner.

Just the same, Hank was a remarkable chap, even if he wasn't the picture of a smart business man and was probably a stranger to the word "personality." He was a success; he was a topnotcher. It wasn't so much that he was his own purchasing agent, salesman, manager, clerk, credit man, and accountant; it was because he knew his public intimately and served it well.

Hank Knew His Customers

He knew more about his customers than Jim Bailey, the barber, did. And he knew the whole community only a little less well than old Doc Knowlton and Mr. Pollard, the local minister, knew it. He knew all about what Al Hawkins' family went through when the dairy herd got sick and died, and what really happened when the Widow Todd's only son ran away from home and showed up again six months later as suddenly as he had left. And in a town where there was never a closed season on the topic of politics, his store was the unofficial town hall twelve months in the year.

Hank's been dead a long time—been promoted—but his ideas of service live on in the world of business. His idea—the one you sometimes see advertised nowadays as "modern, friendly, personal service"—isn't particularly modern at all. And Hank certainly didn't invent it; the idea is as old as the oldest market place and as new as the latest trademark.

When business first began to get away from one-man outfits like Hank's, the notion of serving the public got

45

lost in the shuffle for a while. The customers missed it first. Then management missed it. Then employees missed it. The result is that during the twentieth century one of the great efforts of big business has been to try to get back that friendly glow that Hank and his neighbors used to get out of doing business together. However, it doesn't make any difference whether a business is big or little, it can fail—and sometimes does—when it loses sight of this undeniable fact:

The public can put any concern out of business if the public thinks it is not being well treated.

On the other hand the public can and will make the fortune of any concern with which it enjoys doing business.

Who Is This Person of Many Moods?

First of all, who is this person of many moods—this important John Q. Public we are talking about? It's you and I. Sometimes when we meet him across the counter he is feeling very important; another time he's temperamental. Then, too, we find him by turn friendly, unreasonable, critical, tired, happy, or timid, depending upon the circumstances. When we put this fellow under the microscope we find that he's one person when being served by others and another person when he is doing the serving. He forgets that the very courtesy which he must display to those he is serving will also get quicker and better results from those who serve him.

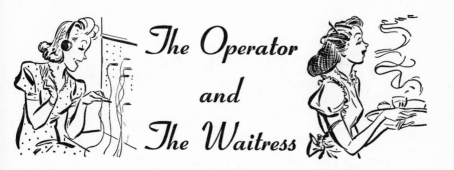

The Operator and The Waitress

For example, a telephone operator (call her Miss Brown) is known as the "voice with a smile," but when she leaves the switchboard and goes to lunch she may "snap the head off" the waitress who fails to get her order right.

The waitress, on the other hand, is the soul of diplomacy while serving cranky customers. She's pleasant, efficient, and tolerant in spite of the treatment she's given. But when two o'clock comes and she takes her relief period, she's very likely to "snap the head off" our Miss Brown if she happens to get the wrong number when making a phone call.

So it goes, depending on which side of the counter one stands. If this chat were written for no other purpose the task would be worth undertaking for the purpose of bringing about better behavior on the part of citizen John Q. Public—making him a bit more tolerant of the feelings of others. It is hard to agree with the statement that the customer is always right— sometimes he's not, and the fact that he is in a position to demand courtesy, tolerance, and a bit of babying now and then whether he deserves it or not should not cause him to take advantage of that situation.

It Would Be a Happier Place

This world of ours would be a much happier place if more patience, greater tolerance, and truer consideration were exercised on both sides of the counter. But, since we can't hope to change this Mr. J. Q. Public very much, we should consider carefully how to handle him so that our jobs are done to the best interest of the firm for which we work.

We've encountered this fellow we must meet and serve, and we know his many moods. Now we'll see how best to handle him so that, regardless of his actions, we won't rub his fur the wrong way and lose a chance for promotion in so doing.

The examples of the telephone operator and the waitress show that we may be on both sides of the counter in one day's time. At work we're serving Mr. J. Q. Public; after hours we are that notable, ourselves. Yes, the public will be served, and the day that it realizes that it is not being served, that day spells doom for the company and your job. Therefore, whether you meet the public personally or through your company's product or service, you should repeatedly apply the Golden Rule: "Do unto others as ye would that they should do unto you."

A Face Without a Smile

There's an old saying that a face without a smile should never open a shop. Let us add to the maxim, "or work in one either." The word "shop" here is used in a broad sense in that it is intended to cover any kind of business contact where one deals with the public from the standpoint of sales, service, or adjustment, either in person or over the telephone.

Many promotions come about because workers have shown by comments, by definite acts, by their whole attitude and point of view, that they had an understanding, not only of their own work and the business of the company by whom they were employed, but an understanding of the public and its needs and rightful demands. I have never heard of a worth-while promotion for anyone who showed by his actions an attitude of "the public be damned."

Harry Smith's first job was that of "office mat" and general utility clerk for the manager of a lumber company. In the course of business Harry had to spend many hours out in the yard where the lumber was graded and shipped. He thought it was the most fascinating thing he had ever seen. He got all steamed up about it and asked the boss if he could spend all his time there. "Yes," said the boss, "if you want to be a lumber grader; but if you want to make good in the lumber business you just do as I tell you—keep your eyes open and learn to meet the public, too."

Each job has its special importance, but all jobs in a single organization are related; nobody deserves a promotion who doesn't understand the relationship between various departments of the operating whole. And nobody can really understand the significance of his own job until he gets an inkling of the part that the business he is engaged in plays in serving the public. Without a real feeling for public service, no man can manage, or sell, or advertise to the advantage of his organization, and he probably will not be given the chance.

We all know what happens when a cat's fur is rubbed the wrong way. The chances are the animal will turn on you and you'll wind up with a scratched hand—you see, the cat doesn't like to have its fur rubbed the wrong way; neither does the public.

The Public Wants Service

If you are now, or later should be, in a position where you contact the public, either for yourself or for someone else, remember this: The person you deal with does not care whether you got out on the wrong side of the bed that morning or not—he is not concerned with your headache, your tired feet, or your family troubles. That customer wants service—prompt, willing service—and always remember that service doubles in value when it is given with a friendly smile.

The manager of a large Chicago store once told his fellow employees: "When you can get customers to come back and insist upon being waited on by you only, you're doing your job right!"

Friendly Service

One of the most successful men in a thriving town of the Middle West attributes his success to one slogan—"Friendly Service." Regardless of when you call on this man, he is never too busy to see you, and every one of his employees seems to radiate friendliness. If you phone his office, you can be sure of a cheery "Good morning" or "Good afternoon." It's not the artificial kind of greeting—it's eager and cordial, and you are immediately impressed with its sincerity. People like to do business with firms and individuals who make them feel important and welcome.

Unfortunately, in spite of the care taken by the management, the public is often ill-treated by those who represent business institutions. Examples of poor public relations on the part of business concerns are common. Here are but a few:

In a Bank

There was a new teller behind the wicket. The bank was crowded and Mr. Stone stood with others in line. When finally he reached the teller's window and presented his check, the teller looked at it and in a rude manner thrust the check back with the remark, "Get it O.K.'d by one of the officers! Next, please." Instead of complying, Mr. Stone SAW RED and told the young man to look up the account himself and he'd find there were funds on deposit to cover the check amply. "You'll have to wait; I can't hold up the entire line just to serve you," was the curt reply. That made Mr. Stone "mad as a hatter," and greatly embarrassed him besides. He immediately reported the case to the president of the bank, who happened to be a member of the same businessmen's club to which he belonged. Of course, the check was promptly cashed, and a new teller was in the cage next day.

How much better and wiser it would have been for that hurried young teller to have said: "Have you an account here, Mr. Stone? If so, won't you just step out of line while I have someone check it? I'll call you when it's ready so that you won't have to get in line again." That kind of treatment would have made a customer, new or old, feel that he was being served to the best of the bank's ability.

In a Large Retail Store

A large store in Chicago advertised in the daily papers a special price on wall tile. The ad read, "22c a square yard." Mrs. McIntire, housewife, saw the ad and realized it was a great bargain. When she went down to place an order, the clerk, who evidently had been besieged with orders at that low price, said, "That ad was a mistake. It should have read 22c a square foot, and anybody with brains or common sense ought to understand that wall tile couldn't possibly be sold at that price."

Well, you can imagine Mrs. McIntire's reaction to such impudent treatment. The clerk probably needed his job, but he lost it within two hours—and you can't blame Mrs. McIntire for making a complaint or the manager for firing the fellow.

How much better it would have been had the clerk said, "I'm sorry. The typesetter made a mistake in the advertisement; it should have read 22c a square foot. You see, it is impossible even to manufacture tile at that figure. However, at 22c a square foot the tile is an excellent bargain—the regular price is 30c a square foot. I'm very sorry that we have caused you so much trouble. Wouldn't you like to order the tile you need at this bargain price?"

In an Automobile Agency

After working all morning to fix his car, Mr. Connors finally laid down his tools and called to his wife. "I'm going to trade this car in and buy a new one RIGHT NOW!!!" Without waiting to change his grease-stained overalls or wash his hands, he walked to an automobile agency owned by a club brother and located about a quarter of a mile from his home.

When Mr. Connors walked into the establishment, the salesman on duty looked him over from head to foot and, not seeing in him a prospect for a new car, remained seated at his desk, completely indifferent to the visitor, while he scanned a file of prospect cards. Mr. Connors, without protest, busied himself looking over the different models. When he decided on the car he wanted, he approached this super-salesman and said: "Young man, are you too busy to sell me an automobile?" The reply to this question set Mr. Connors back on his heels, for, looking the inquirer over again, the fellow answered: "I don't handle used-car sales, and the used-car manager isn't in."

At this point the young man received a jolt! Without further ado, Mr. Connors picked up the telephone on the desk, called the owner of the automobile agency at his home, and said: "Frank, would you mind coming over and selling me an automobile? The young man you have on the job today doesn't want to sell me one until I wash my hands and change my clothes."

How much wiser it would have been for that young man to have been courteous in spite of the fact that the visitor's appearance did not suggest "ready money." The commission for the sale would have been his, and another booster would have been added to his personal list of customers and future prospects.

 *Taking a Credit Application*

A home owner was heard to complain: "I'll go without before I buy another thing on time." The unpleasant experience he had undergone fully justified his statement. He needed a hot-water heater, and since it entailed a rather large outlay of money he decided to buy it from a firm that offered time-payment facilities. The salesman who waited on this man was most courteous and accommodating, but in the credit department the warmth that had been displayed by the salesman changed to a "cold winter breeze" on the part of the credit man who made out the application for credit. Instead of making this new customer feel that he was doing the store a favor by ordering the heater, the credit man reversed the situation. The questions he asked in filling out the credit application were "shot" at the customer in such a manner it made him feel he was going through a third degree.

How much more sensible it would have been for  that credit man to have first put the customer at ease, explained that the credit application was a necessary evil and asked the questions in a warm, friendly manner. Such polite treatment would have been appreciated, and the individual concerned would have become a real booster for the store; instead, all he can think of is getting the bill paid so that he won't have to deal with that firm again.

The incidents cited are not uncommon examples of poor salesmanship. Indifference or impudent treatment at the hands of salespeople and other workers is a common experience. The matter of meeting the public properly is such an acute problem in business today that large stores constantly employ "shoppers" to come in and make purchases in order to check up on the manner in which their customers are treated.

The examples given illustrate a fact you yourself demonstrate every time you do business with others. During the transaction the person you do business with is the company as far as you are concerned. The personal contact is the thing that determines your whole attitude and state of mind toward the concern that the individual represents.

Since this is true, just turn the picture around and try to get an honest snapshot of yourself and your behavior toward those who come to do business with your company.

When You Go Shopping

Perhaps you're a salesman; perhaps you work behind a toilet goods counter; perhaps you receive guests in the outer office of the president; or perhaps you work in the shop. Wherever you are, the rule is the same: Receive and treat the public as you would like to be received and treated.

Here are some suggestions for building up your feeling for public service. When you go shopping, make a game of it. Keep score on the people who wait on you. Ask yourself such questions as these:

Was he interested in what I wanted?

Did he have anything useful or intelligent to say about what he had to sell? Did he try to connect what he offered with my own needs?

Was he cheerful and courteous?

Which Way Do You Look—
Inward or Outward?

"Yes, all that has been said is no doubt true," you are probably thinking, "but what has it got to do with me? On my job I never see this public so earnestly being considered. Look—I sit at that desk over in the corner, and I don't see anybody except our department personnel, month in, month out." Or, "I work 'way down at the end of the shop. The way I look, halfway through a messy job, nobody would want to meet me; and you may be sure I don't want to meet anyone."

That's understandable. It may be true that you are on a job where there's little chance of dealing with the public. But, wait a minute—remember we have been talking about promotion. It's well to recall that the people who run a business are looking for the kind of assistance that will help them, and they will get it from their own staff if they can—and if they're sensible. What does that mean to you?

It should mean that you should never forget to think about the effect of your behavior on the relations of your company with the public. You don't have to be a "public relations" man to grasp that. You simply need to refuse to be mentally shut up inside your job. You have got to force yourself to look outward, not inward.

What's more, your actions on and off the job have a direct bearing on your future with the company. Among your friends, for example, you perhaps are the company—you are the only person they know who works there. Are you a good advertisement or not?

Keep in mind that when you boost your company, whether on or off the job, you are boosting yourself because you are a part of the company. If it fails, you are out of a job; if it succeeds, you succeed. Somewhere along in your job, regardless of where you may be working, you are contributing to the manufacturing of a product or a service that must be sold to the public.

If, by your every word and action, you are doing your level best to see that the product or the service reaches the public in a salable condition and at a price that will meet competition, you are then doing your job as it should be done, for you are meeting the public through the company's product or service, and the public's acceptance of that product or service has a lot to do with your weekly income and with your chances for success with the firm.

A Truism

In all relations with others, try to bring out the best in them. This principle has a remarkable reaction as it will never fail to bring out the best in you.

Teamwork

COOPERATION

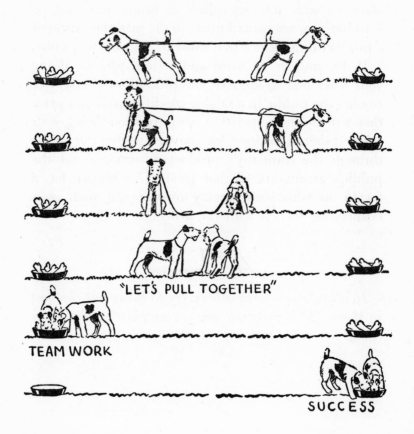

"LET'S PULL TOGETHER"

TEAM WORK

SUCCESS

$\mathcal{T}elephone$
$\mathcal{T}echnique$

THE TELEPHONE, with its many benefits, presents problems that our great-grandparents never had to worry about. Back in those days communications were conveyed by messenger either by word of mouth or by means of the written word. Wrong numbers, busy lines, or a list of "do's and don'ts" for good telephone technique and manners were unknown and unnecessary.

Today a large portion of business is done "over the phone." Therefore, good telephone habits are important to anyone who wishes to prosper in business. And while the telephone, like the automobile, is practically

61

indispensable in modern life, it is at the same time a major source of irritation even under good conditions.

Let's consider some of the reasons for the foregoing statement. Suppose you want to make an engagement for tomorrow night with an acquaintance who lives, say, 15 miles away. If you have a car you can drive over to see him, but that takes quite a while and if you should go the next night, too, that would make two trips—expensive in time and money. You might telegraph, but that also costs money. The telephone

gives you quick, cheap, immediate, two-way communication. You use it almost automatically. And you use it without considering whether it's convenient, at the moment, for the person you are calling to talk with you. He may be waiting for the doctor to arrive in answer to an urgent call; he may be enjoying (or so he expected) an hour's quiet reading he had eagerly anticipated; he may be entertaining a friend whom he hasn't seen for years; he may be doing any one of a dozen things he had hoped to do without interruption. But do you stop to think about these things? Not as a rule.

A Very Necessary Intruder

Why are telephone manners important, then? Simply because the ringing of the telephone is the most persistent and vexatious invasion of privacy that has yet been invented. Abruptly claiming one's attention, the intruder had better be pleasant if he's going to take the sting out of that insistent bell. We may on occasion refuse to answer a doorbell, but it takes iron resolution not to answer the telephone; in short, it's all but impossible.

When that bell rings, we drop what we are doing and pick up the receiver. We don't think about it twice, we just do it. We are the slaves of the bell; and it must be so. Modern business cannot function without the telephone.  But it can be a nuisance as well as a useful servant.

The first consideration, then, is the one already suggested: Remember that many times when you use the phone you are bursting in unceremoniously on somebody's privacy, taking his time, interrupting his work and his thoughts. That bell at the other end rings with a shrill, imperative tone that would not be used in entering a home or an office.

Secondly, don't call a person three times if once will do. You wouldn't go to the office of the chief executive of your company three times a day to talk about things you forgot the first time. But a person's wits often desert him when he reaches for the phone, so that he can think of only one question instead of four or five. It's just as necessary to organize a phone call as it is to organize a letter if you have several points to cover. That habit not only gives you a good starting point, but it suggests a suitable conclusion. If you find that your mind doesn't pick up the points quickly, use your desk pad and make a list of the subjects you want to cover, checking them off in order as you talk.

Plan Your Conversation

One of the most helpful lessons in efficient use of the telephone ever taught came from a rather crusty old engineering executive who had occasion to use the phone at pretty regular intervals. If he had three matters to discuss he would give his name, then say, "I want to discuss three things. First . . ." In this way he gave a clear idea of what he wanted to discuss, but the listener knew the conversation wouldn't be over until all had been dealt with. How often have you received a call from someone and have started to say goodbye and hang up only to hear a frantic: "Here! Wait! Hold on! Here's something else."

So, if you're really going to discuss several points by phone, it's a good idea to give the other fellow some notion of how many topics you have in mind. Furthermore, if you yourself know why you have the phone in your hand, and show it by what you say, you'll have a much easier time getting off the wire when you should. You'll never be a non-stop telephoner if you know when you've reached the end of your story.

How About Your Telephone Voice?

Naturally, purely physical considerations have a lot to do with the impression you make over the wire. It is not necessary to strive for the smooth, honeyed tones of a radio announcer. But it is necessary to be clear and pleasant and to use a tone that isn't flat or "dead." It isn't sufficient to get someone to check on your voice as you use it in casual conversation, because probably it sounds different over the telephone.

It isn't hard to find out whether you are effective or not. The amount and kind of response you receive will show you this. If people keep telling you that they can't hear you, or if you are asked frequently to repeat, you can be pretty sure that the fault is not wholly due to poor hearing or to a "poor connection." You are probably speaking too loudly or too softly; or have

your lips too close to, or too far from, the mouthpiece; or you are not enunciating clearly; or the pitch of your voice is too low or too high—probably the former.

If you have any of these faults, you can correct them with practice. If no one tells you about them and you have any doubts, you'd better ask some of your friends about it or ask your superior, to make sure. An intelligent, friendly switchboard operator can give you many useful hints.

Probably she has been trained by a supervisor from the telephone company and she might arrange to put you in contact with the supervisor if you are interested.

Whatever you do, don't leave the matter to chance. Too much of your business life is going to be spent at the end of a wire for you to be careless about your telephone habits.

It's Like "Mike Fright"

I recall the case of a woman of great charm and ability who had just been promoted to an important secretarial position. One of the most striking things about her was a beautiful contralto speaking voice. But for some reason she had had little telephone experience and her employer soon noticed that her voice, as it came over the wire between their offices, was only remotely like her natural voice. It tightened up for some reason and was curt and almost unpleasant. There was only one sensible thing to do, and he did it; he told her. He couldn't afford to have that voice represent the office to outside telephone callers. She would have to change it. And she did. In that case it was only a matter of being entirely relaxed when she picked up the phone so that she spoke in her natural manner.

Telephone tension of this kind is like what the radio people call "mike fright" (*mike* being short for microphone). In any case, if you feel a tightening up of nerves and muscles, especially in your throat, when you answer a call, make an effort to relax at once. Then go ahead and talk.

Telephone Manners

While on the subject of making telephone calls, let's get in this word of advice. Be nice to the middle man—in most cases, the middle woman. This includes long-distance and local operators and, to come nearer home, the switchboard operator in your office. Yes, they do make mistakes (I suppose you rarely make one!), but they are almost invariably quick, ready, and pleasant in making corrections when mistakes do occur. Even if they are not quick, you will find small satisfaction in venting your own ill temper on them. Patience and civility will get you the best service in the world, year in and year out.

The phone companies have plenty of suggestions on telephone manners, and I have no doubt you can get some pointers from your local company for the asking. Here are a few safe rules that apply particularly when you are doing the calling.

On "outside" calls, be sure you call the right number.

If you get the wrong number, check it in the book

before calling the operator again. Perhaps you made the mistake.

If the number seems to be correct, tell the operator in a pleasant way that you'd like to try it again.

On a dial phone, watch the dial closely and operate it properly to make sure of the connection.

When the connection is completed, it's best to say who you are, even if you think the other person will recognize your voice. If you are calling a company that you have had only casual contact with, give not only your name but the name of your company. (In some cases you will be instructed to give only the name of your company, withholding your own unless it is asked for.) Then state your business.

Be careful not to rush your message. A great deal of time is lost by people who think the "efficient" way to use the telephone is to pour as many words as possible into the mouthpiece in a brief interval of time. You know you can't take messages given in a helter-skelter style, so don't assume that the other fellow can. Give him time to absorb the general subject of your message and then work into it step by step. Take your time and you'll save his.

When you are all through, say "Thank you," and "Goodbye."

If in closing you make some definite arrangement

about a call back, a letter to be written, a bill to be sent, or another call to be made to someone else, make a note of it right then on your calendar, with all details included. If you need to write a memorandum to someone in your firm about the outcome of your call, do it at once, while it is fresh in your mind. Remember that tomorrow morning some of the details may have been forgotten.

Receiving Phone Calls

Now a few words about receiving calls. What should you do when you are the one who is interrupted?

If you are talking with someone when the bell rings, don't swing abruptly away from him. Ask his pardon for the interruption, relax, pick up the phone and give your name in a tone that signifies polite attention. Speak in a natural, easy manner. Maybe you had been feeling tense and "in a hurry." Forget it. Since you have been called, accept the call in the full sense of the word and endeavor to satisfy the demands of the person calling. When the business of the call is concluded, thank the person for calling, if it seems appropriate, and then resume your work. On inter-office calls, the same general rules apply. Relax, be pleasant and sound pleasant. If you will do this, you will find that you can receive unsolicited calls in the light of pleasant interludes instead of thinking of them as irritating interruptions.

You can make friends inside and outside your office if you express yourself properly over the wire. Perhaps the person who calls you from outside doesn't know your name, but he may very well remark to the girl at the next desk, "I don't know who it is up there at the A. B. C. Company, but I surely am glad when I get him on the phone. I can get somewhere talking with him." And maybe a helper down in the stockroom is saying: "Gee, I like to do things for Mr. So-and-so. When he calls down for something he always treats me swell!"

Check Up!

As to your telephone manners, check up by asking yourself the following questions:

When the telephone suddenly interrupts my work, do I show annoyance by my tone of voice when I answer the call?

Am I too talkative in my telephone conversations?

Am I too brief or curt in telephone conversations?

Am I patient with the telephone operator over delay?

Do I speak and enunciate clearly?

Am I ever guilty of taking the receiver from the hook, placing it on the desk and answering when I get good and ready to do so, letting the person at the other end of the wire "burn" in the meantime?

Do I waste my employer's time by making personal calls during business hours?

Do I say "Hello" instead of telling who is talking?

Do my friends and members of my family make a habit of phoning me during working hours?

Do I use tact and diplomacy in giving instructions or orders over the phone?

All of these points are important to remember—whether your present job requires the frequent use of the telephone or not. It may be that when the promotion you are seeking comes along, you may have to use the telephone frequently; if that is true, the way you use it may be a determining factor in judging your value to your company with a view to further upgrading.

Tongue Boners

A TONGUE BONER is anything you may say that causes you to lose the respect or friendship of any human being.

Tongue boners have sabotaged the success of more individuals and produced more business and social catastrophes than have been caused by pressure of the times, accidents, or foul play. Since the reputation we make by the skill and efficiency of our hands or minds may be discounted by the misuse of our tongues, it is well to look into the matter of tongue boners.

Losing Our Tempers

At the top of the list of tongue boners are the things we are apt to say when we lose our tempers. There is one thing sure—when a person loses his temper he loses all around. That is true both in and out of a business establishment. Results are even more deadly in business since it is quite obvious that no one likes to work for or with a person who loses his temper. That being the case, if we aspire to a position of responsibility we must not allow ourselves to get a reputation for not being able to control our tempers.

Jim Evans was a likeable chap—that is, when no one crossed him. When crossed, he was liable to fly into a fit of temper and say some pretty sarcastic things. When it came to making tongue boners, he was a champion. Of course, afterward Jim was always sorry for what he'd said, and he invariably apologized for his cutting remarks. In his mind, the apology straightened everything out again; it did as far as Jim was concerned, but this was not always true of the offended party.

Every now and then Jim was "called on the carpet" and in several instances he came very close to getting his "walking papers." The only thing that saved him was the fact that he was an excellent correspondent.

Then came the time when the office manager was promoted. Jim was next in line in point of years of service, and he was sure that he'd get the job—so sure, in fact, that he went home one night and said to his wife, "You are now looking at the new office manager."

But Jim was wrong. He didn't get the job. His employer just couldn't take a chance on Jim—Jim couldn't keep his temper in a pinch. Jim should have known that no employer will intentionally subject his employees to the abuse of any other employee, regardless of the latter's value as a worker.

Jim was brokenhearted. He knew that for him there was no chance for further advancement in that firm. We all felt sorry for Jim and we admired him when he quit, but down in our hearts we were glad that Jim and his temper were not in charge of the office— what a mess that would have been.

If you are inclined to lose your temper now and then, try this little stunt: instead of saying all the mean, sarcastic things you'd like to say, write them all down on a piece of paper. Take the paper home and sleep on it—then throw it away. You've then had the satisfaction of letting off steam, but no one has been hurt—and, most important of all, you haven't hurt yourself.

Gossip

There's another kind of tongue boner that is just as deadly as sarcasm—gossip—the unkind things we say about co-workers when we engage in a bit of office or shop gossip. To begin with, gossip is the greatest wrecker of teamwork. Once it gets started in any shop or office, it spreads like a cancer, dangerously fast, hurting everyone it touches.

Helen doesn't like Grace, the boss' secretary, or Al doesn't like Pete, the foreman. That's all it takes to start the circle on its deadly way and, as Major Bowes would say, "Round and round she goes; where she stops nobody knows."

We all know that sooner or later the person being talked about finds out what has been said about him. He's deeply hurt, and the chances are that he'll do a bit of "comeback" gossip on his own part. Before it can be stopped there are two warring factions, each trying to enlist the largest group. This may easily result in setting up almost insurmountable barriers between departments—it kills teamwork and results in a "house di-  vided." Many times, too, a person will find that his gossip has become a deadly destructive force that will explode right in his own face, completely obliterating all possible chance for advancement in that firm.

It is a well-known fact that gossip is responsible for a tremendous amount of labor turnover, mistakes, delays, and loss of profits. In some instances, it has been the direct cause of a firm's failure. Some nearsighted individual may say: "What do I care? I'm only working here." Well, let's see if he cares. The individual employee is not something apart from the firm he works for. He is the firm as far as his job is concerned. If by engaging in gossip he causes interdepartment flareups or impedes production or teamwork in any way, he automatically jeopardizes the income of every single individual in the firm, including his own income. So, you see, each and every one of us is very definitely interested in discouraging gossip in any form whatsoever.

Yes, I know it's very easy to get pulled in on a bit of office or shop gossip, but before you allow yourself to become a part of any such gossip session ask yourself these questions: Will what I am saying or listening to in any way hinder teamwork or hurt the feelings of any co-worker if it is found out? If the answer is "Yes," beware; what is being said can affect your pocketbook negatively. If you are not yet convinced, ask yourself another question: Can you think of a single case where it paid to say anything unkind about someone? Can you relate a single instance where talking unkindly about someone has increased a person's pay check by one single penny? On the other hand, we could write a book full of instances where boosting a co-worker, the product, or the company has meant real cash awards.

Don't Get Behind the Eight-Ball

If all this is true, it is clear that gossiping is a vicious practice in which we must not indulge, else we may find ourselves behind the proverbial "eight-ball." Some folks may be willing to listen to a person who resorts to vicious gossip about others; they may even agree with his scoffing remarks; but they will never respect him. Why? Well, simply because they can never be sure that he won't also talk about them as soon as their backs are turned.

A man's success in business entails more than just doing his own job well. Earning the friendly respect of every co-worker is equally important, and no one ever made a sincere friend by saying something unkind about someone else. By indulging in gossip, the back-biter puts the very people he seeks to win as friends on their guard against him. He is shunned, and for the best of reasons.

A Sure Cure

Just in case you find yourself pulling tongue boners—saying things you are not proud of having said about someone—here's a sure cure: Go to the person you talked about and say, "I've been saying things about you I shouldn't have said. Kick me, so I won't do it again!" To be able to do this with good grace is a real challenge. Any such effort, of course, must spring from one's honest conviction that he has committed an offense and from an equally sincere desire to correct the wrong. An open and straightforward approach to the victim of one's tongue boner insures future self-discipline. You most likely will not get a kick, but surely you will stop pulling any more such boners.

Tattling to the Boss

Closely akin to gossip is another tongue boner: The very bad habit of complaining to the boss about co-workers. The person who develops this habit not only loses friends by the score, but the boss soon gets "fed up" with such tactics.

Tattling to the boss is a rather common occurrence in business and, unless the boss is very careful, he may find himself in a very uncomfortable position, especially if he listens to the complaint and acts on it before hearing both sides. The best cure for tattling is to call in both parties and insist that the complaint be repeated in the presence of the person being complained about. Invariably, the complaint is softened—it's not as big as it was at first, and many times the complainer is made to feel just a wee bit ashamed of himself.

Before you make a complaint against a co-worker, be sure that you are willing to make it in his presence. If you are not willing to do that, forget it.

No person working in a shop or office can afford to have a single enemy in the company. It is just as important to be liked and respected by the office boy as by the president of the firm. Ask yourself this question, "Am I the kind of person I'd like to work for?" Answer it honestly; then, just to check yourself, count the people in your firm who like you. Now, count the ones who don't like you. You'd better do something about the ones who don't.

What would happen if tomorrow you were given a new job and only the people who don't like you were to be placed under your supervision? Do you think they would help you to make a success of your new assignment? The answer is "No." Unless you won them over awfully fast, you would fail. They would probably see to it that you did. On the other hand, if they sincerely liked and respected you they would put you over in a big way; they would "work their heads off" for you.

Tongue Boners and the Public

At our lathes, typewriters, desks, or counters, we are all workers serving the public; yet when we leave our places of business to go shopping we become the buying public. The objectionable practices of those who wait on us should teach us how we should act.

As part of the buying public you have at some time or other met all of the characters we are about to discuss. They are as follows: The "steal-the-show" artist, the broadcaster, the bore, the tongue wagger, the snooper, the wrangler, and the scoffer.

The "Steal-the-Show" Artist

The talkative, steal-the-show type of person is irritating and earns the contempt of associates and customers alike. He has the mistaken idea that by dominating the show he attracts attention and displays his "stuff." The important thing he has overlooked is that it sometimes pays to be a good listener. The good listener is the direct opposite of the steal-the-show individual, and he makes friends—true friends. Everybody likes to associate with, work with, and deal with a good listener. It has been said that listening is a great art. It sometimes takes great self-control to be a sympathetic listener, yet it pays real dividends; and that is true whether you are listening to friends, co-workers, or customers.

The Broadcaster

At every opportunity the broadcaster renders an audition on business or social problems and affairs. It matters little to him how he impresses others with his loud voice. He pulls one tongue boner after another. An elderly lady erred in the signing of a check. The check was returned, because of the error, to the store which had accepted it. The girl in the office added insult to injury when she said to the customer who was embarrassed on account of the error, "Oh, you are the one who gave us that hot check. Guess you're not accustomed to giving checks." That young lady was a typical broadcaster. Fortunately, the conversation was heard by the proprietor of the store, who immediately apologized for the employee's bad manners and, as you can readily imagine, it was the young lady's last broadcast in that establishment—she was dismissed.

The Bore

The bore is the individual who is constantly broadcasting his personal affairs. His personal problems are uppermost in his mind and they become the first consideration in his daily contacts.

A newcomer to a small southern city met the assistant cashier of one of the city's banks at a church social. The cashier had a very pleasing personality and in a friendly way he invited the newcomer in to see him at his bank. It so happened that this man was buying a business in this city and had a cashier's check for twenty-one thousand dollars which he desired to deposit to open an account in some good bank. Therefore, he accepted Mr. Hamilton's invitation to visit the bank, his purpose being to arrange for an account and deposit this check. However, Mr. Hamilton's conversation quickly drifted to his pet subject—his family troubles and his problems with his mother-in-law. The prospective customer became so bored that he left—left without opening an account. How many people do you know who fit Mr. Hamilton's description and bore you to death with talk about their operations, their families, or how hard they have to work? The sure way to lose friends and customers is to bore them with your problems.

The Snooper

It is quite natural that customers should ask questions. They want to be sure they will be satisfied with their purchases. However, they avoid clerks who ask personal questions and business houses where such questions are asked. They shun the question artist who is more or less SNOOPY. An interrogation should be worded with great care. Discretion should be used as to the grouping of words and tone of voice.

A man walked up to the perfume department in a Los Angeles department store and asked for a bottle of Caron's Bellodgia perfume. "For your wife?" asked the saleslady. "None of your business!" replied the customer, and he walked out of the store. Another striking incident when the customer thought the clerk was snoopy occurred when a well-to-do woman entered a smart men's shop in Minneapolis and asked to see something in a man's sport coat, size 37. "May I ask who it is for?" asked the salesman. "No, you may not!" came the reply of the customer, and she turned and left the store. In this case the salesman did not intend to be snoopy. What he wanted to know was whether she wanted a coat that was suitable for a young man or a middle-aged gentleman. The question was asked in such a way that it sounded snoopy to the customer. The clerk had pulled a conversational boner that lost business for his firm. Had he asked if she had in mind any definite color, material, or style, she might have answered something like this: "Something suitable for a middle-aged man." Asking questions is a ticklish job in any office or place of business, and we should avoid being SNOOPY or even SOUNDING SNOOPY.

A receptionist in a large chemical plant said she spent many evenings in grouping words to formulate questions she was compelled to ask at her desk, then practiced for many hours speaking aloud the questions so that she would use the proper tone of voice as well as the proper words. This is an excellent plan. She discovered that such practice was not only helpful for the next day's work, but it also developed her sensitivity to the feelings of others. This trait has proved an asset to her even outside her office hours.

The Wrangler

The king of conversational blunderers is the wrangler. He is sadly lacking in diplomacy and creates active dislike in customers and associates by always wanting to set them right. "Aw, you're nuts!" is one of his favorite expressions. "That's where you're wrong," "These are the facts," "I know what I am talking about," are more of the wrangler's pet expressions. The public and his co-workers soon have his number and become "fed up" with him very quickly.

The Scoffer

When jobs are plentiful and help is hard to get, the long-suffering public must put up with the scoffer. Knowing he is desperately needed, he takes full advantage of his independence and gives full sway to his arrogance. As part of the buying public, you have met the scoffer many times. During the war, when asked for some article not available, or for better service, his pet expression was, "Don't you know there's a war on?"—or some other offensive remark. Unfortunately, this individual was not always the waitress, clerk, or man who performed some service for you. Sometimes he or she was the owner of the business you were dealing with. Will you continue to patronize that individual or the company he represents? Probably not; human nature being what it is, you will remember this rude treatment. Someone said that fortunes and reputations are made during wars and depressions. I suppose that is due to the fact that during trying emergencies our true personalities will out. If we work hard and attain a position of importance when we are most needed, we are likely to retain that position of importance; if we abuse the power intrusted to us, we lose it.

The Tongue Wagger

Customers avoid shops and offices where tongue waggers are employed. Discussing transactions that occur in business is dangerous and sometimes becomes the "Judas kiss" that leads to business crucifixion.

An exclusive ladies' shop enjoyed the patronage of men who purchased expensive lingerie and fine hosiery. One afternoon one of the elite women of the city, the wife of a prominent lumber dealer, was making a purchase in this store. The clerk waiting upon her said, "Oh! I bet you were thrilled with those beautiful pajamas Mr. Foster bought the other day." Mrs. Foster froze up like an icicle, snarled, "What pajamas?" and hastily left the store. This BONER caused such a stir in the community that the shop lost the patronage of its entire male clientele.

Consideration for Others

The kind of person you like to deal or associate with —the courteous, unaffected, sincere person—is the successful individual who loses himself or herself in promoting good. This type of individual has a very definite cash value in this business world of ours. He never allows himself to become intoxicated with success. He is never overbearing in conversation or condescending in manner. Such persons are humble, happy, kind, and you get real pleasure out of working with them or dealing with them. They never use their family, an associate, a friend, a customer, or employer as a door mat; they never trample upon the feelings of anyone. They seldom take offense because they never knowingly offend. Moral philosophy, under the heading of gentleness, says: "Kindness is the velvet of social intercourse. Kindness is the oil in the cogs of life's machinery. Kindness is the controlling spring which holds back the slamming door. Kindness is the burlap in the packing case of every day's merchandise. Kindness is the carpet on life's floor which deadens the sound of shuffling feet and adds warmth to silence. Kindness is the touch of an angel's hand."

Success depends on courtesy, openmindedness, devotion to purpose, and consideration for our fellow man in both actions and speech. Remember that a real gentleman never gives offense—not even to those who can never conceivably be of service to him. Be kind, and tongue boners will never handicap you on your road to success.

PART II

Self-Management

The ladder of success is full of splinters but you notice them only when sliding down.

Leisure Time

FEW SUBJECTS are so surrounded with defenses as this subject of "our own" time. We are so afraid that somebody will meddle with it that often we don't even do anything about it ourselves. We let things slide. We take it as it comes, with little thought or planning as to what we might do with this time that we so jealously claim as our own.

Nevertheless, if you don't train yourself to use your own time to your own advantage, and if you make no deliberate plans regarding it, your conscience will give you a twinge every so often. That is, it will if you are at all interested in making your life more interesting, more productive, and more successful.

You have seen that there is a great variety of things to do on your own time. Any one of them, and certainly all of them together, will have telling effect on your worth and effectiveness as a person. As far as

Of 100 men starting out at the age of 25

Out of the average group of one hundred men starting out at age 25, only five will become either wealthy or comfortably fixed by the time they are 65 years of age. The use or abuse of leisure time will determine to a degree into which of these groups we fall.

40 years later

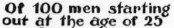

One will be wealthy

4 will be comfortably fixed

5 will be self supporting

54 will be dependent

upon others

These are insurance statistics taken from a folder published by William F. Hochfeldt, insurance broker, 175 W. Jackson Boulevard, Chicago, Illinois.

36 will have died in the meantime

the subject of this book is concerned, you can realize by this time that special skill will take you no more than so far unless you have the personal qualities to back it up. That is why most of the second part of the book deals with matters that are of importance to you as an individual.

What is *leisure?* Why, it's that portion of time in which you are at liberty to *choose* what you will do.

HEALTH. Let's begin by agreeing that the time spent in sleep is, generally speaking, a matter of your own determination. In preceding paragraphs this period—an average of eight hours a night—was duly scheduled. But, on the basis of experience, an allotment of eight hours might be challenged. For it's plain that *if you prefer,* if you feel that you can "get by with it," you may average a great deal less than that. If you are between the ages of 20 and 30, you no doubt feel boundless confidence in your ability to get along with only a few hours of sleep—you may even boast that you can. Perhaps you have read about Thomas Edison's custom of sleeping but a few hours a night and have said that you can do the same.

Edison aside, it won't do you any good to reduce your efficiency by robbing the pillow. You steal something from your own strength, you cut down on the amount you can give your employer the next day. And although you may pretend you are "just as good" as if you had rested a sufficient length of time, you will fall behind the procession sooner or later unless you conserve your vitality. If you sleep less, Nature will force you to work less. It's true there are emergencies, illnesses, interruptions of all kinds in your schedule of rest. But remember—you will be less ready to meet such emergencies if you have no nervous and physical reserves upon which to draw. Such reserves are built up on a schedule of regular hours of sleep that is given first place on the list of health-building activities.

Since your job probably keeps you shut up indoors much of the time both winter and summer, you should plan some activity that will keep you outdoors for part of your leisure time. According to your own tastes and opportunities you may swim, skate, hunt, fish, or play baseball, golf, or tennis. Or perhaps you prefer long walks. Whatever you do outdoors, the time you spend at it is precious. It strengthens your lungs and muscles and keeps your body toned up and in sound health. Physical fitness is an obligation.

At the same time, most workers should remember that they are not professional athletes. They should not try to go in too heavily for sports on a week end after five or six days of comparative inactivity. Too much or too violent exercise is worse than none at all. For example the person who is not used to strenuous exercise and who goes to a picnic, runs races with the young folks, plays ball, and goes in swimming all in one day, usually is headed for trouble. Even if he doesn't suffer exhaustion, he is sure to be "muscle sore" for the following week and in no fit mental or physical condition to render efficient service to his employer. Know your capacity for physical exercise and take it in the proper doses.

Have a Hobby

Many inventions and important improvements have their beginnings in hobbies. In fact, it is said that the discoveries made by enthusiasts in experimenting with model airplanes have contributed considerably to the improvement of both commercial and fighting planes.

One of the foremost authorities on diamonds in this country took up the study of diamonds as a hobby. The inventor of the Kiddie Kar made his first model for his own child in the basement of his home, where tinkering was his hobby. Neighbors who saw the toy wanted cars like it for their children, and thus a toy manufacturing concern was started.

It was Darwin who said: "Have a hobby, but don't follow it for profit. Use it as a means of relaxation." While many hobbies have resulted in definite financial gains, it must be remembered that they cease to be real hobbies when profits accrue through them. Hobbies may take the form of collecting various items such as miniatures, or of building models or tinkering with power tools—but whatever the hobby is, it should be something you really like to do which is also something different from the things you work at to earn your living.

Of course hobbies can be overdone as everyone knows. There's that chap across the street, for ex-

95

ample. He builds miniature trains and he says that unless he watches himself carefully he'll work night after night in his workshop until the wee hours of the morning. And most likely after going to bed he'll lie awake planning what he's going to do the next evening. He realizes that this is not fair to his job because he's bound to feel tired starting out the next morning. It would be much smarter, he decided, to watch the clock in his workshop than to watch it at the office in anxious anticipation of quitting time.

By all means HAVE A HOBBY—but he sure that you find in it a real source of relaxation, and—don't overdo it.

You probably "ride your hobby" alone; you like to talk about it with those who share your enthusiasm; still it's rather a private interest, too, and satisfying of itself. You are missing something, however, if you follow a private hobby so closely that you avoid society and social occasions.

SOCIAL ACTIVITIES: The hours of leisure you spend in fellowship with your friends are highly important. In them you develop your personality, snap the workaday tension, and build up reserve energy for the next day—that is, if you use these hours wisely. You can't sit at a bridge table or dance until midnight, night after night, and expect to be alert and "on the job" the next morning. To do so is to *abuse* your leisure hours—not *use* them sanely.

In your social hours, also, you get the chance to develop yourself in directions that will be of immense value to you in business. Among friends you have a fine opportunity to show qualities of cooperation, loyalty, and leadership. This word "social" means just what it says; it is the very opposite of the word "individual" or "personal."

Therefore, if you are truly social, you forget yourself and your personal affairs and troubles, and throw yourself into the interests of your friends and acquaintances as far as it is possible or proper to do so. Naturally, getting used to the other fellow's point of view is necessary in business; but hardly in less degree is it necessary in useful and happy living. And the chances are that unless you feel your hours outside business are happy and useful, you are going to have a hard time feeling happy and useful in your work.

So, for practical reasons, and for reasons that you may call idealistic if you like, you should plan to reach out toward the interests of other people during part of your leisure time. Does someone want to plan a benefit? Or collect money for some community work? Or plan a dance or a dinner? Then you be first to show some interest and help. Or, better still, you be the one to propose new activities and try to get people as enthusiastic as you are.

Such efforts are all the more necessary if you have been looked upon as something of a shrinking violet and have been in the habit of withdrawing from people. Almost all of us at some time in our lives have heard a voice inside us say "Oh! I could *never* do that!" or "What! Before *all those people!*" or "Oh, no! I'd be too frightened."

If you sometimes hear that voice yourself, don't worry about it. More than likely the people you admire most for their ability to work with others and their capacity to enjoy group activities were not born that way.

At one time probably they felt just like you—self-conscious, or even fearful in social situations. As a matter of fact we are not born social. We *develop* into social beings. And about the surest way to develop yourself socially is through working and playing with your friends. It takes you out of yourself and gives you a slant on experience which you can get in no other way and which also is practically indispensable to your business progress.

PURSUIT OF EDUCATION: Your leisure-time program is not complete without a good deal of conscious planning for extension of your education. Everything so far mentioned, of course, affects your growth and development. Everything we do carries us in one direction or another, forward or backward, keeps us on the right road and shunts us onto a sidetrack. We never stand still. We are always changing. The question now to be considered is, how far are we able to control or direct the changes that affect us? Perhaps our work helps to educate us, broadly speaking, and perhaps it doesn't. It all depends on the job. But in

part of our leisure time we can make some kind of plan that will help us expand and grow. In fact, almost our only chance of controlling our future lies right here—in using part of our leisure for study and constructive reading. Newton D. Baker, once Mayor of Cleveland, later Secretary of War, said: "A man who graduates today and stops learning tomorrow is uneducated the day after." It doesn't happen as quickly as all that perhaps, but it is surprising how rapidly we can slip back if we let our minds become inactive. No engine can run at top speed constantly without wearing out before its time, but an engine that is habitually idle rusts beyond serviceability and exists to no purpose.

The easiest way to plan your hours for study is simply to ask yourself in which direction you would like to go. What do you most need to know that will be of probable advantage to you in the future? When you know the answer, do something about it without delay. Look around you. The problem now is not "What am I going to learn?" but "How? And from whom?"

In America, fortunately, these problems are easy to solve. In most cities schools and colleges offer academic and vocational courses to people who are employed during the day and are therefore unable to attend day classes. There are library facilities, too—helpful to resident school students and correspondence school students alike. And there is an increasing amount of educational and vocational material being offered on the radio.

In your case, however, it may be that the programs of study offered in local or near-by night schools do not include a course in the subject you wish to pursue. (This is often the case with respect to vocational studies.) And, for the employed person, there is always the problem of suiting one's free time to designated hours of attendance in class. As for radio material, it may be found too sketchy and superficial to be of large benefit to the serious student.

In view of these considerations, probably your best chance of increasing your fundamental knowledge and skill lies in wide reading and in pursuing study courses designed specifically for people who must further their education at home in their leisure time.

If you use books alone, do all you can to make sure that you get the best, and devise a method of organizing the various topics in your mind so you can get the most out of every book you read. Start first with

 your local library. Get the advice of the librarian. If there are not sufficient books on hand on the subject matter you desire to study, make a list of titles and ask to have the books borrowed from a larger library. This is done by what is called the Inter-library Loan Service. That is to say, you can't borrow from an out-of-town library yourself, but your local library can do so. When you secure the books look them over carefully and, as soon as you can afford it, buy those best suited to your needs and add them to your personal library. Borrowed books are almost indispensable to a study program, for few of us can afford to buy all the books we need for study purposes. But the foundation books —the most important ones—these we should own and keep in a place close at hand.

SPECIALIZED STUDY: Wise selection and practical use of books in a study program call for a good deal of training and experience on your part. You are practically sole organizer and creator of your own course of study. In a regularly organized home-study course, on the other hand, the selection and organization of material for study purposes is done for you. Your efforts are both directed and criticized as in any other course, and you receive guidance from your instructor on additional books and materials to use if you wish to broaden your study. Probably organized home-study courses are the most thorough and efficient means now available to those who cannot attend resident schools.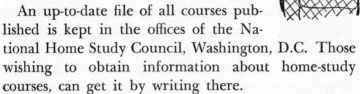

An up-to-date file of all courses published is kept in the offices of the National Home Study Council, Washington, D.C. Those wishing to obtain information about home-study courses, can get it by writing there.

As to the value of home-study courses, we find that our leading correspondence schools number among their graduates such men as the late Walter P. Chrysler, Fred S. Deusenberg, Captain Eddie Rickenbacker, and other national figures of industry. Then too, we find, upon looking into the records, that some of our leading statesmen and educators are graduates of home-study institutions.

According to an article which appeared in the August, 1939, issue of *Future Magazine* entitled "Ten Million Alumni," by Roth Wyrick, one outstanding home-study school listed among its graduates the Governor of Georgia, a United States Senator from Michigan, the attorney general of Vermont, the executive director of the Chicago Association of Commerce, a district attorney from New Mexico, the controller of the United States Gypsum Company, a professor of Harvard University (since deceased), the auditor of the Goodrich Tire and Rubber Company, the president of the A.P.W. Paper Company, the controller of the city of St. Paul, the publisher of *Opportunity* magazine, the business manager of *Popular Mechanics,* and the Dean of Engineering at the State College of New Mexico. Remember, these prominent men were all students of only *one* home-study school.

If you want to win promotion you must fully appreciate the value of "spare time" study and make use of the splendid opportunities available. Adopt a well-thought-out program of self-improvement—seek knowledge about the job you are doing today and the job you hope to do tomorrow.

This chapter, you may have noticed, has been full of spur to action. But constant drive isn't the whole story, by any means. Take time out to think, to reflect, to let your mind wander. Life isn't all flurry and bustle. A story is told of a busy executive who went to see an oculist about his eyes. The doctor examined him and when he finished he shook his head and said, "You don't need glasses." "But, doctor," the executive protested, "I have to read many hours every day. It's quite a strain, you know, as much of it is very close work." The doctor grinned and replied, "Well, can't you stop and look at the horizon once in a while?"

We all need to take time now and then to look at the horizon. It improves our perspective of our jobs and our lives. To the goal of ultimate development of our potentialities do we *work* and *play* and *study*—each in its special province, each in its right proportion, *all* for the greatest realization of SELF.

Getting Personal

YOUR SPEECH, your looks, your actions—these are the means by which you express yourself to the world. There's a saying as old as the hills that puts it thus, "It doesn't matter what you *seem* to be, it's what you *are* that counts." Well, of course, nobody is going to argue that point with you. There's also another saying about potatoes by Robert Frost, one of our modern poets, which goes something like this: Some people pretend to like their potatoes covered with mud and dirt, but most people like their potatoes clean; inside its always the same potato. You may have a heart of gold, but you don't show your heart to many people. On the whole, they're not interested; but they are greatly interested in your manners.

Your manner of speaking comes first. It's not exactly an easy subject to write about, and it might better be demonstrated in a few practice sessions. There are, however, several practical suggestions which you can apply in studying and correcting your own habits of speech.

103

First, it's right to warn you against adopting the language and manner of speaking you hear on the radio in many adventure and comedy programs. Most programs of this kind contain at least one character who speaks roughly and ungrammatically in order to be in character. The dialogue of the script was written that way intentionally so it would sound "natural." This is not an attempt to tell radio dramatists their business, you understand. The thought is that if you are a *habitual* listener to such programs, your habits of speech will suffer—unless you've been thoroughly drilled in correct grammar and good habits of speech. Dialect and slang phrases are funny when used in moderation. They are a real handicap if you use them habitually.

Comic strips are another case in point. Not all, but a great many strips depend on misspellings and various corruptions of usual forms of speech to lend color to the characters presented. If you read these strips day after day, you will unconsciously get the notion that there is something fine and democratic about the lingo of the heroes and heroines of the funnies. Don't be misled. Don't try to be an actor out of the comic supplements or out of a radio program. You won't sound very amusing, and you may corrupt what was originally a very good manner of speaking.

Not long ago a famous essayist wrote that people get together largely to hear each other's "tunes." He said that each of us has a characteristic "tune" when we speak in conversation, and this tune is what other people know us by. They listen to it, or turn away from it and shut their ears, according to whether they like the tune or not.

Your personal tune is made up partly of the language you use, partly by how you pronounce words and how you enunciate, and partly by the control, or modulation, you employ in speaking. To effect this management of voice sounds like a big order for a mechanism that began function long before you were able to read or write; nevertheless, a surprising number of people make a low score when it comes to their everyday speech. They may be very bright people; indeed they frequently are; but it's something of a trial to listen to them just the same. It's hard for the speaker himself to get an idea of how he sounds, but other people know. So if you don't get free criticism about the way you speak, I advise you to ask for it from some friend who knows you pretty well or whose speech you admire. You may not like what you hear—but you'd better pay close attention to what is told you.

Here are some important don'ts by which you can make an attempt to check up on your habits.

Don't mumble, *but*

Don't speak ten times louder than is necessary to make your audience hear. In business offices there are bawlers and shouters, and there are whisperers. It is a common experience in offices to have people come up to within a yard of where one is sitting and speak as if they were giving commands to a company of infantry on drill. Other people call at the office—salesmen, too, mind you—who speak so low one has to lean forward, listen hard, and do a little lip reading to make out what they are trying to say. In general, if the

muscles of your throat and jaws are relaxed, and if you breathe evenly and naturally, you will get a good, full tone. You can gauge the proper volume of tone by several things, namely, by the size of the room, by the expression on the faces of those to whom you are speaking (strain or other discomfort on the part of the listener is easy to detect), and by echoes of your voice as they bounce back at you sometimes if you are talking too loud. While we are on the subject, it may be well to warn you that science, in its effort to kill irritating noises, has developed soundproofing insulation to a high degree. If you enter an office that is so insulated, you must watch yourself. Sound-insulated walls absorb noises to such an extent that an ordinary conversational tone sinks into them like water into gravel. Usually, however, offices are so arranged that your worry is not the unusual quiet, but how to make yourself understood while using a subdued tone of voice.

Don't use slang habitually, or try to make your talk "snappy" and "bright" by making it coarse, as in comic-strip style. A good command of conventional language is absolutely essential to your progress, whether in speech or writing. Do the things that will build up such command—not those that will tear it down.

Don't get angry if someone corrects you on pronunciation or other points connected with speech. Check up on the criticism, and if it seems just and unbiased, make a change. Even highly educated people have their blind spots when it comes to pronouncing and using words.

Don't make the mistake of depending on profane speech and a store of off-color stories for your reputation. They'll give you a reputation beyond doubt, but not the kind you can use to advantage.

Don't forget that there are several people in the circle of your acquaintances to whom you like to listen. You feel gratified and refreshed after a talk with them. To a great extent this salutary result is produced by the manner in which these individuals speak, so you'd better see if you can't adopt some of the good habits of people you admire.

Don't forget that speech is very largely a matter of imitation, so pick your models with care. When you were a baby, you imitated the sounds your parents and other members of your family made in speaking to you, and you found in time that the sounds you made had meaning for others. Now that you are older, the number of your models is greater. You have as good a sense as anyone of what is fine in speech. Set your mark high and try earnestly to reach it.

Don't—whatever you do—*don't* try to pretend. An affected, unnatural way of speaking is so painful, it's funny. Try to fit your words and your tone to both yourself and the situation in which you happen to be involved.

Don't try in your business conversations to drag in a lot of information and ideas that are interesting in themselves but totally irrelevant to the subject being discussed. Talk about business when business is the concern, and talk about it in the clearest, most direct way you know how.

CLOTHING: Your speech is part of your "dress," if you like to think of it in that way, but your clothing itself is very important indeed. This problem, thank goodness, isn't as serious as it was in days gone by  because of the fact that designers and tailors of our time can create garments that, though made of excellent materials and beautifully styled, are at the same time moderately priced and admirably suited to practical needs. Furthermore, fashion guidance has been developed to a point where you can safely rely on the trained personnel of reputable stores to guide you in your choice of appropriate and becoming clothing. If you go into a store and state the purpose for which you want a particular garment and name the price you have in mind to pay, it will be unusual if the salesperson in attendance fails to give helpful advice. Nowadays salespeople are trained in points of special service to customers. Particularly on occasions when you feel uncertain as to the suitability of a garment for specific use, as for business wear, will you act wisely in consulting a style-informed person in a store known to be reliable.

To receive the greatest help from salespeople be absolutely frank on *price,* and state the need the garment is to serve. This practice plus your own common sense will give you a business wardrobe that is comfortable, becoming, right in style and reasonable in price.

When you have acquired an appropriate wardrobe, take good care of it. Keep every article clean, in repair, and neatly ironed or pressed. Attention to such matters suggests that you respect yourself and also that you wish to appear well in the eyes of others.

Getting Very Personal. In the chapter "Office Talk," we discussed personal cleanliness quite briefly. It is important to understand, however, that the matter of personal hygiene is by no means important to office workers alone. It is of vital importance almost any place where people work in close proximity. The basic thought behind this matter of personal cleanliness is consideration for others. When we ignore this plain duty, we pay the penalty in one way or another. If we believe that to succeed it is necessary that those with whom we work must boost for us, then good personal habits are seen to be very important.

The person who unwittingly, day after day, offends others because of lack of attention to bad breath or body odors, becomes a real problem in office, store, or shop. The problem is not an easy one to solve without deeply hurting the offender's sensibilities. This is especially true if the person seems not to be aware of his fault. Many times a whispering campaign started by fellow workers reaches a serious point before the management can step in. Unsympathetic fellow employees may go so far as to leave notes or verses about "B.O." on the desk of the offender, with perhaps a bar of soap or a bottle of cheap perfume by way of suggestion. You can readily imagine how the recipient of such treatment feels. In most cases, the person's feelings are so hurt that he quits then and there.

Fortunately, in most cases, employees complain to the department head about offenders instead of taking matters in their own hands. When such a complaint is made, the management is faced with a difficult problem. No matter how diplomatically the matter is handled, the offender is deeply mortified. Very few persons are thick-skinned enough not to be extremely embarrassed in cases of this kind. Usually the only way the person can recover his self-esteem is to quit, sacrifice his chance of success with the company, and seek another job.

The purpose of this discussion is to point out the pitfalls that can retard and even wreck careers. Carelessness with respect to personal hygiene is one of those pitfalls. It has caused much unpleasantness to those offended, and seriously hinders the progress of the one who offends. It is easy to understand, then, that one cannot take lightly the duty of personal cleanliness, for success hinges upon this trait quite as much as upon one's efficiency on the job.

We do not all wear white collars in our daily work, but regardless of the kind of clothing one wears, one must be careful to look neat and clean. The people we like to work with are the kind who are considerate of others in all things. Sloppy Joe habits do not lend color in office or shop. On the contrary, they lend an air of laxness that signifies poor management. That being the case, department executives keep a watchful eye out for the careless employee. In view of this, it is vitally important to check up every morning before leaving for work to be sure that one has neglected nothing that would make one unacceptable to others.

A word more about clothing. It is not necessary to be a Beau Brummell, meticulous in every detail of dress, but it is only good sense for persons working in offices and stores to use care in selection of their clothing. It is better to have two suits of high-grade materials and good styling than to have four or five suits that are obviously of poor quality and perhaps ill-suited to practical use.

Women office workers will many times display poor judgment by wearing dresses that seem out of place—dresses that are, in fact, entirely unsuited to daytime wear, wherever worn. This bad practice will sometimes be defended on the plea of desiring to look feminine. It is not the "feminine" but the "fanciful" that is decried. There is no lack of feminine appeal in the good-looking casuals designed for business wear—trim, well-styled dresses that are youthful and smart, but never fussy.

Keep in mind, then, that fuss and feathers are not for nine to five, not for the workaday atmosphere of store or office. Your taste in matters of dress, remember, is indicative of your personality. Discernment, a sense of the fitness of things, is no small factor in personal success.

Hitching Your Star to a Wagon

DREAMING ABOUT THE FUTURE gives our lives added interest and power. We have all read about the apparently miraculous progress and success of certain individuals who realized some of their dreams even after starting under very unpromising circumstances. But what good would Edison's dreams have done him if he had not possessed—and used untiringly—a great inventive talent? And what would have become of Lincoln's political dreams, if he had not used and developed his extraordinary gifts for political debate and decision? You know the answer. Under other circumstances, Edison and Lincoln might have become ineffective, disappointed men.

To make your dream come true, there must be some relation between what you dream of becoming and what you habitually do. Perhaps merely making this assertion is like throwing a bucket of ice water on you; but a cold plunge is sometimes healthful. Probably you have met women, and men, too, who think they ought to be, or would like to be, movie stars. At least they say so, but it is clear all the time that either they do not have "what it takes," or they are unwilling to undergo the risks and the heartaches attendant on realizing such an ambition. In short, it's not an ambition at all—it's just so many words that have no relation whatever to reality. The same is often true of those who say they would like to be writers. It's significant that they do not say they like to write, or that they have to write—merely that they would like to be writers because they have heard of the fame and fortune won by a few novelists. They envy the rewards without thinking of the means by which the rewards are achieved.

A certain young man was, so he said, deeply interested in airplane design. He was sure he was going to work up in the industry and become a dominant figure in it. The only hitch was that he had a hard time understanding mathematics and physics. He disliked them. He wouldn't study. He wouldn't pay the price of connecting his abilities to his dreams. His dreams in that direction bore no relation to his situation or his ability. He *had no wagon to which to hitch his star.*

Now, perhaps, you can see why this chapter does not deal with intangible things such as ambition, will-power, etc. Ambitions and dreams are an important part of everyone's make-up, but they are tricky things to handle and direct. In fact, the surest way to get a clue to a person's qualities is by looking at his external behavior. You may have earnestness of purpose and the ambition of Alexander the Great, but these qualities are not going to be of use to anyone, yourself included, except as they receive impetus through action. You may, as you believe, have a high degree of intelligence, but it will do you no good if you fail to put your intelligence to the proper use, or if you regularly draw the wrong conclusions in situations that arise from day to day.

This chapter might have been headed simply "Finding Yourself" or "Discovering Yourself," because that is what you do whenever you make the right tie-up between your intentions for the future and your present abilities and habits.

You often hear people—especially young people—talk as if this process of finding one's self were something that took place once and for all. The younger people are, the more likely are they to believe this is so. The twelve-year-old is quite sure that when he grows up he is going to be a cowboy. He is certain about it, and will not argue the point. And his family no doubt lives in a three-room apartment a thousand miles or more from the nearest ranch. When he is 16 years old, he has forgotten all about steers and horses. Then he wants to be something quite different, perhaps a salesman, or a preacher, or an interior decorator. And he is just as sure as he was before!

Not all young people are like this, but most of them show rapid shift in interest. Sometimes, indeed far too often, this changefulness lasts until long after the person is of voting age. And then you can see some heartbreaking cases if you are in the right place to observe them. For a man, let us say, 30 years of age who has not yet found his proper work has not yet found himself, and he can get very much confused and discouraged. In a way you can't blame him. He feels he has spent ten or more years of his working life in running up blind alleys. He thinks of many things he might have done, decisions he might have made, years ago, that would have changed his life for the better. He thinks of his family. He thinks of the effort it will take to change his affairs for the better. He may even come to think of himself as an old man at thirty! An attitude of defeat forms as a man begins to view his past life with regret.

You may be sure, however, there is no need of your getting into such a state of mind, or anything approaching it, if you will act according to three easily understood ideas.

FIRST. *Your career is not something wrapped up and delivered to you in a neat package like a suit of clothes.*

SECOND. *Become accustomed to making any changes in your habits that changing developments may indicate.*

THIRD. *The most responsible and successful men and women are those who have a broad mental outlook.*

Let's take the first idea first, and see what it means. We all know men who apparently are born to carry on the business, trade or profession started or followed by their father and grandfathers. But in our modern world, especially considering the ease with which we can move about the country, this sort of thing is the exception. We hear a lot about the "disappearance of the frontier," and it is true that the frontier in the "Wild West" sense has disappeared. At the same time, Americans have just as much of an "itching foot," a desire to experiment, and to see and learn new things, as they ever had. We can get around the country more quickly, easily, and economically than ever before. We have more information about what is going on in different regions and in different lines of commerce and industry. These are facts nobody will deny. And for the person who wants to test out his abilities, to use them to the greatest possible extent, and to accustom himself to many different kinds of conditions, the chances were never more favorable than now. *All depends upon the individual.* It is certain that anyone who does not want, or does not dare, to do any of these things has no good reason for reading a book of this kind. He has no *personal frontiers* to explore or new conditions to meet.

Did you ever stop to wonder about the thousands of people who can't hope for promotion, simply because they don't realize they are in a line of work to which they are unsuited? Or of the thousands who "make the best of the situation," that is, do nothing about it?

Oh, we know how it is, all right. We sympathize. A job's a job in any man's language. How do I know I'm going up the wrong alley? Besides, it's too much work to try to change over. And think of the risk!

These arguments have been used many times, never more forcibly than by a brilliant young man named Bert—not so young, either—say in his early 30's. He did his work creditably, but it was obvious to his superior he was in the wrong place. Why? Because he was "settling down," in the bad sense of the expression. Perhaps settling *back* would better express what was happening. He wasn't studying his job. You could tell by looking at him he wasn't going anywhere. *In his imagination he was already there. He had arrived.* Yet it was plain he had used and was then using only part of his powers. It was not his fault so much as the fault of the job. He was told he ought to quit and get into a different line—just enough different to restore that sense of growth and progress he had shown only a few years back.

No, he'd bought a house; he had three children; the risk was too great; he was doing well enough, etc., etc. His employer took a chance on his judgment, told Bert he was about through on his job—and, for the time being, won a sincere enemy. But it worked! Bert began to grow and thrive again, in the new work  suggested. He sacrificed considerable income for a year or so, but eventually more than made up for it.

One of the great needs and lessons in modern life is to be found in the phrase, *progressive adaptation.* These words may sound scientific and uninteresting, but they describe the process by which millions of us, yourself included, manage to make a living. Progressive adaptation calls for a continual study of yourself and of the general movements of business and industry, so that you can keep pace with developments. It's a simple plan in mere words, but actually a hard one to work out, unless you are keenly aware of the necessity for doing so.

In the movies, in museums, and in newspapers and books, you have seen pictures of the huge and terrifying animals that perished millions of years ago because they could not adapt themselves to new conditions of living. Today scientists find their skeletons and reconstruct them for us to see and think about—the mastodons and the pterodactyls, and the strange creatures with even stranger names that A. Conan Doyle pictured in his book, *The Lost World*.

In the history of our own nation we can find examples that strike nearer home. For instance, you have read books and probably have seen many movies on the subject of the great wagon trains that moved across the country during the last century. The people in those trains left their homes, their native towns, and many associations dear to them. But as they moved, they left something else behind, too. They left whole communities stranded on unprofitable hillsides, in fever-ridden bottom lands and in swampy country, as well as in unlovely shacks on the edges of little settlements. Why were these people left behind to suffer from the effects of fever, starvation, and generally poor conditions for themselves and their children?

The reasons varied with the individual family, but the underlying reason was the same: *They couldn't keep up*. They couldn't adapt themselves, physically or mentally, to the demands made on them by a wagon

118

train moving on into a dangerous, largely unknown, but certainly more desirable country than that in which they decided to stay. Please do not interpret this as a scornful or unfeeling comment on some of the western pioneers. The historical record is used merely to illustrate a point which is becoming more important to you, rather than less important, now that we no longer have to make up a wagon train to get where we think we want to go.

Almost every day we see some article in a paper about how rapidly the world changes. We are likely to read it and nod approvingly, and say, "Yes, the world sure does move." Unfortunately, too many of us fail to realize that as our world moves, we must move with it. Every serious depression, or any other great social disaster, tells the same story. After the market crash of 1929, many brokers and others who depended for their livelihood on trading in money, and stocks and bonds, were wiped out financially. Some suffered severe physical and mental distress as a result. And little wonder! They had been deprived of income from the one skill they knew. Many became permanently deranged. Some committed suicide. The demonstrated fact was that these men had lost the power of progressive adaptation.

In several great industrial areas of our country, examples of the same thing may be found easily. Suppose a man is an expert garment cutter. He makes fine wages. He risks his future on his one skill. He makes excellent wages when the shops are busy, but he may have long periods of no employment and no income. His future depends almost entirely on forces over which he has practically no control. His skill, however superior, limits his progress unless he consciously determines to create for himself a broader sphere of activity.

The same thing is true in anthracite coal mining, in steel, and in other areas of industry. Progressive adaptation is perhaps a still more urgent matter where semi-skilled workers are concerned. And all men, financiers, managers, skilled, semi-skilled, and unskilled workers might come to the point where they could make no further progress. But under the worst conditions, as under the best, the individuals who overcome obstacles are those who attempt to adapt themselves to changing conditions and opportunities. The fact remains that you can take advantage of *new* frontiers in business and industry today, if you have a real pioneer spirit, if you are alert to opportunities through your own live interest in events and changes and your consistent effort to keep up with your world.

As you go on in life, bear in mind especially that any decision you may make in business is not necessarily the final decision. You are always a free agent to a certain extent. If you should make the wrong start, almost always you can make another start in a new direction. It isn't any *one* decision or any *one* act that makes the final difference, but the whole trend, the whole pattern, that decides the outcome.

If you are twenty years of age now, the chances are you will be doing something different when you are twenty-five. And that will be all right if you have used your will and your intelligence, and have capitalized on opportunities as they were presented to you. A young man once complained to an older friend that a certain venture had turned out badly, after he had had great hopes for it. Naturally, since he wasn't the person affected, the older friend took the disaster more calmly than the young man did. He thought at the time that his friend ought to sympathize a lot more than he did. But he had cause to remember and appreciate what the more experienced man said. His remark was in the form of an old saying: "All is grist that comes to the mill."

Maybe you never went into a grist mill. There used to be one wherever a river could turn mill wheels. People would bring corn and wheat and rye from miles around to be ground between the mill stones. The miller would take any kind of grain and grind it for a fee. It was all grist to him, no matter who brought it, no matter what kind of grain it was.

If you examine every experience you go through, think honestly about it, and then keep going, you will not suffer actual loss, although you may feel at the time you are losing ground. Most successful men "go through the mill" in many ways. They acquire many different skills and interests you would never guess by merely looking at them. One successful man was a sailor, a novelist, a clerk, and a manager, before he "settled down" at a time some would call "late in life" as a first-rate advertising man. Another was an immigrant who couldn't speak the English language when he landed in this country shortly after his twenty-first birthday. Now, a little more than twenty years later, he has three degrees from some of our best universities, and is a remarkable teacher. The next time you

121

read a "success" story, pay special attention to the different kinds of experience, the amount of *progressive adaptation* that the hero of the story can lay claim to. You will probably find he has had an amazing range of experience, has held a number of different jobs, every one of which has been "grist to his mill." Men have been born to become kings, and women to be queens, but no one can be born a future president of the United States. If you ever get to be president, and a good one, you will have been through many experiences that molded your character, and made you stronger and wiser than you were before.

In order to make your development real and effective, you may often be faced with the necessity of making major changes in your own customs and those of your family. Geographical location becomes especially important here. Frequently, of course, illness or some other handicap may keep a man from moving from one locality to another where he expects to be able to do better. Furthermore, opinion in a family may be divided, whether the husband, a son, or a daughter is the one who wishes to make the change. Almost all conservative people are against ventures of this kind. The expense involved, the friends left behind, the risks in a new place, all these are arguments brought to bear against a change. And it cannot be denied that these are powerful factors, but at some time you may have to face these arguments and take the risk of deciding against them in favor of the benefit you believe can be gained by cutting loose from your old moorings. If your plans happen to turn out wrong —why, then you'll have to make the best of it. The important thing is that you do not lose your willingness to experiment, and that you base your experiments upon an intelligent estimate of your own powers, and of the situation you are investigating.

Again, change in your customs may be necessary because you have set out on a long-term program of study and reading to prepare yourself for some new kind of work, or a more responsible job. This project, sincerely adhered to, may disarrange your present schedule and provide irritations and discomforts that not only you, but your family as well, must be reconciled to sooner or later. Some companies will train you on company time—but very few will *re*-train you on the same kind of time. What you do in the way of adapting yourself through further education must come out of your own budget of leisure; specifically, out of the time you have been in the habit of giving to your family and close friends. For this reason, when you attempt any extensive educational program, get the full cooperation of your family, if you can. Otherwise, it's not going to be easy to change your customary leisure time habits for the sake of a benefit you hope to receive in the future.

If you become discouraged in studying alone at home, you may be helped by remembering you are by no means alone in your method. You are one of a great army of men and women all over the country who have tried to bring their abilities into relationship with their dreams, and are doing something every day to make that relationship more effective. You can picture them in libraries, on trains, and trolleys, in evening and Saturday classes, and in their rooms, working constantly and finding themselves *progressively,* through thought and study, turning part of their leisure into their greatest chance for growth and progress. They have seen their star some time before. Now they are hard at work making a wagon to which they can hitch it.

Don't be afraid to change your *locality,* or your *habits,* or your *job.* This last perhaps takes more nerve than either of the others, especially if you live on a pretty narrow budget. But sometimes it is necessary to do just that, if you are to realize the best that's in you.

Many folks are surprised—always agreeably—by the number of people who possess just this type of nerve. A well-to-do salesman, a man sixty years of age, was talking recently to a friend about his career. In part his story went something like this: "I had worked for years and years for a certain company. I did all kinds of things for them. I didn't like it much, but every job I had was a pretty good one. So I stayed on and stayed on. And then, all of a sudden, it came to me one day about ten years ago [he was fifty then!] that the company and I weren't really doing each other any good. So I resigned—just like that."

At fifty years of age he found his vocation, has made a success of it, asks only for the privilege of "dying in harness," and is one of the finest, most serene, and happiest men you'd want to see.

Suppose he had waited until he was sixty? Then the story would probably have had a different ending. The only point is: Don't be afraid to jump. If your *real* opportunity, or what you have reason to believe is your opportunity, entails throwing up a job, then take the risk. *But never do anything of this kind in a fit of temper, or merely because you want to see how the sun sets on the other side of the hill. We can tell you beforehand that it sets in just the same way.*

Think, analyze, plan—and then act. After all, it's your career, and if you don't think about it, not many others will take the trouble to do so for you.

Now we come to the third point—the *quality* of the men and women in responsible positions. Whole books have been written on this subject, but everything we want to say about it now can be said in a very few pages.

We hear a lot—a lot too much—about "stuffed shirts" and "brass hats" in business and industry. You will be interested to hear what an authority on business has to say on this subject: "Perhaps I haven't gone to the right places, but in fifteen years of traveling around the country I've not yet met anyone in a responsible position on whom I'd try to fit a brass hat or on whom I'd hang the label of 'stuffed shirt.' And I've been interested to meet this fictitious character, just as all of us would like to meet Sherlock Holmes, for I've heard so much about him. I've looked everywhere I could—in offices, on trains, on ships at sea, on vacation trips, in hotels, at dinner tables. And I have never met a person with any claim to distinction at all, on whom I could justly pin the label. Little people who have done little and talked much—yes; others who have done nothing and talked still more—yes; these are the 'stuffed shirts.'

"But the people who had won their responsibilities and were discharging them, who had a vision of their work and were fulfilling it—of these, there was not a 'stuffed shirt' in the lot." Two qualities of these remarkable people which are memorable link together all the things pointed out heretofore.

They have solid confidence in the importance of their work, and therefore they desire to do it well. They feel it is important not only for themselves, but for society as a whole.

The second quality is this: *These people have a greater range than the average.*

Now what is meant by *range?* When the word is used in relation to a rifle, it means how far it can shoot and still hit a target. When used in relation to traveling, it means how far a traveler has gone in many different directions. When used in relation to a person's mind and interests, the word means the number of interests and the quality of understanding which the person brings to each.

Let's take, as an example, a successful real estate man —not an officer of the company but a competent man in his job, earning a really surprising amount of money in what you might call a minor executive capacity. To begin with he has spent his time for some thirty years, on the job and off, learning his field. He knows a great deal about finance, and enough real estate law to hold his own with most lawyers. He knows the main points in the building codes of his city. Having done a lot of selling, he knows the desires and foibles of commercial and domestic tenants. He has picked up an amazing knowledge of the trades associated with building. He knows good masonry from bad, and when plumbing and electrical work are properly installed. He is always doing committee work for the local real estate board. He helps to supervise a settlement house. He works on at least one civic committee each year.

These, you say, are all more or less related to his work. True. But ten other men, or more, with a position like his can be found without any trouble, who don't have a tenth of his range.

Furthermore, he happened to become acquainted in his youth with some great music—the music of Beethoven. It opened a new world for him, and he spends as much time as he can spare listening to fine music. He has made many acquaintances in the world of books as well. Perhaps you wouldn't guess it, as you look at him behind his desk. He's a bit on the heavy side, has thin gray hair, smokes cheap, rather violent cigars. But the more you talk with him, the longer you know him, the more you realize that this old codger (not really old—only fifty or so) has *range*—a good long reach.

He has kept alive and alert. He is an authority on his work, but still keeps learning more about it. He has rich experience outside his job as well, which is probably worth to his company as much in dollars and cents as his professional knowledge. Personal growth, personal *range,* isn't a matter of knowing how to keep up small talk on cultural subjects; it's a matter of a deeper and wider understanding of your fellows.

Don't lose any chance to increase your *range*. That's the biggest part to the job of hitching, not your wagon to a star, but your star to a wagon.

PART III

Selling Yourself

Through self-management we learn the art of managing others.

OLD PHILOSOPHER 1940

How to Find a Job

FINDING A JOB is an experience common to virtually everyone; for some, the experience is repeated many times. Since the problem is one of selling oneself to an employer, the surest way to succeed is to start with the right attitude.

How shall we describe what the "right" attitude is? It has a great deal to do with thinking about the needs of the other fellow—in this case your prospective employer—about which a good deal has already been said. But the job-seeker, particularly if he is young and ambitious, has special problems of his own, and he will have to go through a process of adjustment before he can hope to succeed.

A common criticism of young college graduates is, or used to be, that they think the world owes them a living. If a young fellow feels this way, he gets the feeling knocked out of him before long. But the feeling isn't by any means confined to college graduates. The fact is that almost *anyone* who has thought and studied hard to prepare himself for a job he hopes to get is likely to have a false idea of his own importance on completion of his course.

It is necessary, for example, for you to take your career pretty seriously and to spend a lot of time preparing for it. However, unless *your own* plans and hopes loom pretty large in your mind, you will not do this. You've *got* to be self-centered, or you won't generate enough steam to carry yourself along. You *must* feel that you are important, to build up the courage and endurance to push yourself ahead.

 Nevertheless, when you come to the stage in your training where you think you are able to go out and sell your abilities, then is the time when you have got to make a right-about-face in your mental attitude. Just at this point you are relegated to the background in the picture. You have become a *seller*. The *buyer* is the person upon whom attention centers. You must concentrate not on yourself but on him. Easy to *say*—hard to *do*—but *absolutely essential* nevertheless.

What doesn't the buyer, your prospective employer, care about? Well, he doesn't care about your career. He doesn't care how hard you may have worked to prepare yourself for it. He doesn't want to hear all the details of your personal history nor about your aunts and nephews and cousins. *He doesn't care whether you get a job or not. That's your worry.*

Of course, he is interested in the bearing that these and other personal matters have on your fitness for service to his organization. He's glad to know that you're ambitious, that you come from a respectable family, that you have taken thought for your education. But understand, he's interested in these things only insofar as they give him a picture of you. What he wants is a person who will join his staff and perform stated duties cheerfully and ably for some stated compensation. Everything that he seeks to find out about you turns on the single point of your usefulness to him. If you appear to have qualities that suggest the possibility of advancement later on, well and good, but that's another story. Most jobs are got not on the basis of a satisfactory answer to the question, "What can you do five years from now?" On the contrary, they are likely to depend on the reply you make to the question, "What can you deliver tomorrow morning at nine o'clock?"

With this thought in mind you had better check over carefully the wares you can deliver to your prospect if he hires you to work for him. It's not altogether easy to make a true estimate of one's own abilities, but if you stick to facts, if you tell what you have actually *done,* then you won't go far wrong. These facts will later find their place in letters of application and in sales talks you will use when you are interviewed.

One purpose of this book is to outline a plan you may use in securing employment. *Plan* is the important word. Don't neglect it. If you are going to write a letter, organize it before you start to write. If you are going to see a man in his office, don't wait until you face him before you start thinking about what you will say. Arrange your story beforehand, memorize it, and practice it on your family or friends until you can talk easily and naturally, without embarrassment. Only then are you prepared to "speak your piece" to a stranger amid strange surroundings. Planning will give you self-confidence and will show the person who interviews you that you have *thought about your qualifications in terms of his specific needs.*

Just one more reminder before outlining the job campaign. *Never under any circumstances go into an office or shop and merely ask for a job.* Instead, offer yourself for some specific kind of work which you believe you are qualified to do. The weakest advertisement in the world is the one which ends, "Will do anything." This no doubt shows an amiable spirit of cooperativeness, but as selling argument it is fuzzy and weak. To sell yourself you must have something concrete to offer and a single goal which you are attempting to reach.

Pounding the Pavement

The most generally used plan for finding a job is that of tramping the streets, calling on one factory or office after another, asking over and over again the same question: "Are you hiring anyone?" Behind this plan is the hope that the Goddess of Chance will take care of the searcher, and the belief that if one calls on enough people one is bound to strike an opening. This might be called the Pounding-the-Pavement Plan. It is really no plan at all; it shows no analysis of the problem. It is, in fact, a *retreat* from the problem, not an intelligent *attack*.

SELLING YOURSELF

In looking for a job, the situation is one of merchandising. You are selling a definite product, i.e., your own knowledge and ability, and your success or failure will depend upon how well you merchandise your abilities. Therefore, since finding a job is a matter of merchandising, follow the plan used by many successful business firms, and let the United States mail carriers do your pavement pounding.

This plan consists of writing letters of application to a selected group of prospective employers. In case you feel that this means of finding a position is perhaps hopeless, just remember this: it is the only plan which gives you an opportunity to get your story across to the man higher up. In following the recommendation that you adhere to the plan presented in this and the following chapter, be assured that it is a sensible one—tried and found workable.

There are three definite steps in the plan proposed, namely:

1. Building a mailing list of prospective employers
2. Selling yourself by letter
3. Selling yourself in a personal interview

BUILDING A "BUYER" LIST

Naturally, the only buyers for the product that you have to sell are employers. Therefore, the first thing to do is to get a complete list of prospective employers —that is, a list of firms in your community or near-by territory for which you would like to work. These prospects can be secured from a number of available sources.

First: Note the business firms listed in your local phone directory and in the directories of towns within a reasonable radius of your home city. Your public library or your Chamber of Commerce will generally have commercial reports on these firms, from which you can obtain information as to classification of business as well as the firms' financial rating. The librarian will show you how to find this information.

Second: Inquire about firms newly located or seeking location in your territory. Your Chamber of Commerce can give you the names of such firms. These, of course, are splendid prospects.

LISTING FIRM NAMES

List your names systematically. The form shown here is recommended. Note that the form includes spaces for noting the date of first letter, date of second letter, and details of reply. When you write your first letter to a prospect, be sure to put down the date, so that you will be able to carry on the follow-up procedure suggested on pages 139 and 140.

LETTERS TO PROSPECTIVE EMPLOYERS

Firm Name_____

Address _____

Executive's Name_____

Date of   Date of
  1st letter_____2d letter_____

Details of reply_____

_____

_____

In the following chapter letters of application are discussed and outlined.

The Letter Campaign

THE "BLIND" LETTER OF APPLICATION forms a topic of chief concern in this discussion. Having secured a list of prospective employers, you are now ready to approach company officers for the purpose of securing an interview. No one will hire you "sight unseen," so remember that these letters have only *one purpose,* i.e., to gain entry to the office of your prospect.

Probably the best way to approach staff executives is to circularize them with a "blind" letter of application. (The letter is called "blind" because it is sent to prospective employers who have not advertised for help.)

The letter must get the employer's prompt attention, stimulate his interest in you, and create a desire on his part to see you and talk with you personally at an early date.

A suggested outline for such a letter is presented on the following page.

138

OUTLINE NO. 1

Date

Name of firm
Address of firm

Attention of:............, (TITLE)

Gentlemen:

1. Opening	State your desire to become connected with the firm.
2. Personal	Give certain personal data, your age, whether married or single, whether you have children, whether you are in good health.
3. Education	Describe briefly your previous training and education. Name any special courses you have recently completed or are now studying.
4. Experience	Give a condensed outline of jobs you have held, with dates.
5. References	List three personal references. Get permission to use these names and say in the letter that you are using them by permission. Be sure to include the addresses of persons given as references.
6. Request	Ask for an interview.

(Signature)

Yours truly,
Name
Address
Telephone number

Below is an example of Outline No. 1 filled in.

EXAMPLE

Date

Name of firm
Address of firm
Attention of........., Manager

Gentlemen:

1. It is my sincere desire to become connected with your organization, preferably in the bookkeeping or accounting department, although any position open at the present time that later may offer me the opportunity I am looking for, will be welcome.

2. My qualifications are: Age——; unmarried; good health; high-school graduate.
3. In addition, I am a graduate of college extension work in Business Administration. This training is practical as well as theoretical and covers bookkeeping, auditing, cost accounting, accounting management, sales, advertising, production and financial management, commercial law, credits, collections, and kindred business subjects.
4. My employment record is as follows:
   May 1937 to December 1939—James Steel Company, Chicago, Ill., time-keeper—bookkeeper—auditor. December 1939 to November 1940—Sears, Roebuck and Co., Chicago, Ill., bookkeeper in credit department.
   Detailed record will be furnished on request.
5. Attached are the names and addresses of three character references.
6. May I expect an early interview, with the understanding that it implies no obligation on your part?

Very truly yours,
Name
Address
Telephone number

Following Up
"No Opening"
Replies

In selling by mail, as in calling in person, the prospect is not always sold on the first approach. Therefore, it is necessary to have a follow-up system.

The following letter outline is designed for cases wherein the employer has replied to your "blind" letter, saying that there is no opening at present but that he is filing your application for future reference.

Note: Always address this letter to the person who replied to your previous letter. Mail 30 days after date of employer's reply.

OUTLINE NO. 2
(Same salutation as in original letter)

Paragraph 1   Thank your correspondent for his courteous response to your application.

Paragraph 2   Say that while there still may be no opening for you, you would be pleased to be granted an interview so that he (the person addressed) can be given a definite impression of you to judge whether you merit serious consideration when an opening does occur.

Paragraph 3   Repeat the personal and educational data given in the first letter, varying the form slightly.

Paragraph 4   Ask for an interview within the next week or ten days.

(Signature as before)

FOLLOWING UP "NO REPLY" TO FIRST LETTER

The outline presented next is designed to follow up employers who did not reply to your letter. The list of prospective employers you have prepared is a "live" list and is certainly worth more than one follow-up. Do not consider that the prospect is "dead" just because you received no reply to your first letter. Another letter may reach the mark. In fact, with this plan of approach, the second letter sometimes produces better results than the first. Therefore, you should certainly make another attempt to get a reply. Mail this type of letter 30 days after your first letter.

OUTLINE NO. 3

Paragraph 1   Refer briefly to the date and purpose of your first letter. *Do not* sound disappointed or

141

aggrieved at not getting a reply. Above all, *don't* say you are "surprised" not to have heard.

Paragraph 2   Say that while there may be no opening at present you would like a chance to talk with your correspondent, etc., as in Outline No. 2.

(Follow Outline No. 2 for remainder of letter)

Answering Help Wanted Ads

In addition to circularizing your own mailing list of prospective employers, you can approach other "live" prospects by answering Help Wanted advertisements published in local or out-of-town papers. Many of these ads are run "blind"—that is, with only a box number as the address.

Most of these Help Wanted ads specify the kind of opening that is available, and your qualifications must, of course, meet the specifications of the ad. This type of letter is much more interesting to write because it gives you an opportunity to do a better job of selling your training and ability.

OUTLINE NO. 4

Follow the pattern of Outline No. 1, with two important exceptions. First, Paragraph 1 should state that you are answering a specific ad. If you wish, you may cut the ad out and paste it neatly at the head of your letter for reference. Second, after you have stated what experience you have had point out how your abilities and experience fit you for the job named in the ad.

IMPORTANT POINTS ON WRITING A LETTER OF APPLICATION

In making application for a position by letter, you should bear in mind that your letter represents YOU. You would not think of applying to a prospective employer looking dirty, with your clothes wrinkled and soiled, and your shoes crying for polish. That is, you would not do this if you were interested in securing a position. It is just as important that your letter should look well and make a good impression.

Don't use business stationery when writing about a job. Many employers are prejudiced against the employee who uses his firm's stationery—and perhaps its postage stamps—in his private correspondence.

Don't use note paper or hotel letterheads. They are out of place in business correspondence, and generally are too small for business files—a fact which may cause your letter to be mislaid or lost.

Use plain white typewriter paper, of good quality, size 8½x11 inches. This is the standard size for business stationery.

Use a plain white envelope to match your letter sheet. If you are enclosing letters of recommendation, etc., use the legal size envelope, 9½ inches long; otherwise use the commercial size, 6¾ inches long.

If requested to answer in your own handwriting, use ink, and make your handwritten letter look as neat and business-like as possible. A "good hand" is required of persons who keep records or make reports, therefore, a handwritten reply may be requested to

143

show the quality of your penmanship, but a specimen of your writing may be sought also as evidence of your education and general ability.

If your own handwriting is not specified, have your letter and envelope neatly typewritten if possible. The cost is trifling, while the impression given is that you are familiar with business methods.

Write on one side of the paper only; and, if your letter runs over two pages, see that the pages are plainly numbered at the top.

Always sign your letter in ink. A lead pencil, typewritten or rubber-stamp signature betrays ignorance of business methods.

Keep a duplicate copy of your letter—a carbon, if it is typewritten. You may want to refer to it later on.

Be sure that your name and address are given plainly, both in your letter and on the envelope. Put your address and telephone number at the bottom of the letter, directly below your signature.

Be sure that your letter carries sufficient postage, and contains a stamped and self-addressed envelope for enclosure of any matter you wish returned.

Preparing for an Interview

Let us assume that an employer, in response to one of your letters of application, has suggested that you present yourself for an interview. It's very natural for you to want to "drop everything and run," getting there as fast as you can; but that's the wrong thing to do. There's work to be done before you make that call.

First, if you haven't found out facts you ought to know about the firm you hope to become associated with, do so before you call. Important facts are:

a)   The business of the firm.
b)   What goods they produce or sell.
c)   The length of time they have been in business.
d)   Their financial rating.
e)   The kind of a job you are to apply for.
f)   Your qualifications for that job.

All of these facts are important—they will form the basis of the sales talk you will use to secure a position.

Don't grope your way into a job. That's Point No. 1. Surprising as it may seem, few job seekers take the trouble to look up anything about the companies to whom they apply for positions. They seek jobs blindly, trusting to luck. (See page 136.)

Point No. 2 is even more important. Employers generally would be eagerly attentive if a young man or young lady were to come into the office and, instead of using the old hackneyed, threadbare question, "Have you any openings?" or "I'm the man you wrote to," they would speak right up and say: "My name is Henry Smith. I am calling in response to your letter." Then, after presenting your qualifications, continue: "I am somewhat familiar with your firm. I know that it has been in business for forty years, that it is AA1 in Dun and Bradstreet, a leader in its field, and the kind of concern I'd like to work for, etc."

145

That kind of approach, because it is direct and intelligent, creates a favorable impression.

The following form will be of help to you in compiling and recording this information.

INFORMATION ABOUT PROSPECTIVE
EMPLOYERS

Name of company_____

Address _____

City_____ State_____

Dun and Bradstreet's rating_____

How long in business?_____

Nature of business_____

_____

What territory do they cover?_____

_____

Name of owner or president_____

_____

Name of person to whom application is made_____

_____

His title_____

Miscellaneous information about firm or product they
sell _____

_____

_____

What kind of job do you want with this firm?_____

_____

What are your qualifications for this job?_____

_____

_____

_____

Study the above form carefully.

Note: It has two important functions: (1) it allows you to familiarize yourself with the firm to whom you are applying for a job; (2) it makes you stop and think, first of the kind of job you are seeking and secondly about your qualifications for that job. Most people wait until they are face to face with a prospective employer before they give these matters proper consideration. As a result they are nervous, they stammer, throw facts together in a disorganized manner and naturally make a poor impression on the prospective employer.

It doesn't take very long to compile the facts suggested—an hour or two usually—but however long it takes the time will be well invested, for you will have gathered essential facts on which to build a sales talk that will sell YOU.

Discussion of the personal interview will be presented later on, but before we get into that topic there's one more item of preparation to be considered. This is the urgently important task of gathering data for the application form you will be asked to fill out if you are to be considered for the job in question.

Prepare Your Application Beforehand

Most folks overlook this important detail and, as a result, when they are given an application form to fill out they become nervous, their minds seem to go blank, and instead of writing the application neatly

APPLICATION FOR EMPLOYMENT
(SHORT FORM)

Date of Application	Position Desired	Department

Full Name of Applicant	Age	Post Office Address in Full

QUESTIONS	ANSWERS
Are you single or married?	
How many persons, if any, and who, are dependent upon you?	
Do you own or rent the house in which you live? Do you live with relatives, or do you board?	
How long have you resided at your present address?	
Where did you previously reside and how long?	
If now employed, what position do you hold, and what salary are you receiving?	
If now employed, why do you wish to leave your present position?	
If out of employment, what is the last position you held and at what salary?	
If out of employment, why did you leave your last position?	
Have you ever been discharged from any employment? If so, give particulars.	
At what salary will you accept a position?	
State what education you have had, and from what school you graduated.	
Are you a member of any church, if so, which; and if not, what is your religious preference?	
Have you ever applied for a bond to a bonding company? If so, were you ever refused the issue of such a bond?	

(Back)

APPLICATION FOR EMPLOYMENT—Cont.

Below state name and address of your parents or other nearest relative.

Name	Relation	Occupation	Address

Below give the names and Postoffice address in full of three or more persons as References—not previous employers—who are well acquainted with you and who are not related to you.

Name	Occupation	Postoffice Address in Full

Below give full particulars of your occupations or employments during the past five years. Give full disposition of your time for past five years, whether employed or not.

From What Date	To What Date	Nature of Your Position or Occupation	Place Where Employed or Located	Name of Employer and His Present Address	Why Did You Leave
Month	Month				
Year	Year				
Month	Month				
Year	Year				
Month	Month				
Year	Year				
Month	Month				
Year	Year				
Month	Month				
Year	Year				

and quickly they make mistakes, write poorly, and give a bad impression of their true abilities. This is especially true when it becomes necessary to fill out the application under the eye of a prospective employer.

Don't leave this detail to chance. Prepare all the facts beforehand. Write them down on a card and take the card with you. As to facts you will need, study carefully the application form shown on pages 148 and 149.

There are many types of application forms in use today. Some are as short as the one shown. Others are four or more pages in length. One firm, for example, may use two or three different types of applications, one for office workers, one for factory workers, and another type for their sales organization.

Regarding applications used by sales departments, these may include questions of territory covered, fraternal connections, hobbies, and reading habits, and provide space for detailed reports of the kinds of products you have handled and the types of prospects you have contacted.

However, if you have at your fingertips the information required in the short form illustrated you will be well prepared to fill out any application form that may be presented.

Keep in mind that when you fill out an application for employment you are doing the first job asked of you by an employer. The manner in which you perform this first task attests your abilities. If you do the job neatly, in reasonable time, and take

150

pains to write plainly and avoid erasures, you will make a good impression.

Often prospective employees will ask for a second application form, explaining that they made an error on the first one. In other cases, applications are handed in only partly filled out, or with answers to questions written in the wrong places on the form. Again, important dates are omitted entirely. You may be sure that such applications find their way into the wastebasket—they aren't even filed for future consideration.

Compiling beforehand the data you will need to fill out an application form properly achieves another result. It calls to mind important facts to use in the sales talk you will make later.

SELLING YOURSELF AT THE INTERVIEW

We have heard many times that a chain is only as strong as its weakest link. Apply this rule to business and you will find it equally true that a business is only as strong as its weakest department.

Up to this point you have been in the business of selling yourself by mail—that is, your ability and training. Thus far you have laid your plans carefully. Your advertising department has secured a fine list of prospects which it has circularized;  you now have some "live wire" prospects (tentative employers) who have requested that you present yourself for an interview; you have investigated the firm and you are prepared to fill out an application.

Your next problem is one of direct selling, and,

since the close of the campaign depends entirely upon how well you sell yourself, it is not only advisable but necessary that you prepare your talk beforehand.

Your first reaction to the suggestion that you prepare a sales talk in advance will be a very natural one —you will say you are afraid a prepared talk will sound stiff and unnatural. You are right; there is that danger unless the talk is your *own*, every word of it. You think the whole thing through, and write down what *you* think. You try it out on the folks at home, and on one or two close friends, who give you helpful suggestions and do not hesitate to point out faults of grammar or pronunciation. This criticism is just what you want. You make notes of every comment and every suggestion so that later you can work in necessary changes. The "try out" of your talk enables you to watch reactions as you emphasize certain points.

If you like to sing you will agree that you can put variations in a song you know really well. But when you sing a song you are unfamiliar with, you are too busy concentrating on the melody to attempt variations. The same is true of a sales talk. When you know it thoroughly you can deliver it effectively and with ease, putting emphasis where it belongs and making the talk a convincing story of your abilities and qualifications.

Doesn't careful preparation of this kind sound like common sense? The real value to you in preparing a sales talk is that it requires you to do some real thinking; you will have to arrange your data and put down all the facts about yourself. Having done this there will be no embarrassing pauses, no groping for words. And you will have a much better chance of getting your message across without interruption if it has form, that is, if it is put together in a presentable manner, with all details arranged in their proper order.

What about interruptions? You will, without a doubt, be interrupted in many cases; therefore it will be well for you to anticipate interruptions so that when they occur you will not lose the thread of your story and appear helpless in your effort to pick it up again. The minute you are interrupted, make a mental note of the point at which your talk was broken off, and when you are given a chance to proceed, you will generally find you can do so without difficulty.

How to Plan Your Sales Talk

You have already developed two sources of information from which to draw in building your sales talk, namely, the data you secured about the firm to whom you are applying for a job and the data you have compiled for filling out your application for employment. Now that you are starting to build your talk you can readily appreciate how important these fact-finding tasks are.

First let us give our attention to an outline of the sales talk and then later fill in the data.

THE OUTLINE
1. Name of the person who is to interview you.
2. Give your name.

3. State that you are calling in response to his letter.
4. Give your age, nationality, education.
5. Mention any advanced training you have had or are now taking.
6. State your experience.
7. Tell what kinds of work you are interested in.
8. State your qualifications for that work.
9. Present in brief outline your knowledge of the firm, its products, etc.
10. Offer to furnish reference.

Let's see how it looks when the outline is filled in.

EXAMPLE

Mr. Morgan, my name is Herbert Brown. I am calling on you in response to your letter of June 3, in which you suggested that I drop in for a personal interview. I am 22 years old, an American, in good health and graduated from high school five years ago. In addition to high school work, I have completed on my own time a course of training in Business Administration that covered sales, advertising, production, accounting, commercial law, finance, and statistics.

Two years ago I was employed as bookkeeper for Langston Ellis of this city. I left the firm to work for Kreig & Co., also of this city, as second assistant manager in charge of buying. As you know, that firm went out of business last month.

I am seeking a position with your firm preferably in the accounting department, although any position open at the present time that eventually would enable me to get into that department would be welcome.

I am familiar with both single and double-entry bookkeeping, trial balance procedure, posting, statistics, and cost accounting.

My previous experience and study equipped me for this type of work.

I am somewhat familiar with your firm and its products. I know it is rated A+A1 in Dun and Bradstreet and that it is one of the outstanding firms in its line. In other words, it's the kind of concern I'd like to work for *permanently*. I can furnish character references if you

154

desire, and you will find that I am an earnest and reliable worker. All I ask is an opportunity to prove my ability.

Remember the example given is merely an illustration—an outline, to be used only as a guide. Be sure your talk is your own, that it represents *you*. Talk as naturally as you would to a neighbor. Never enter an office and reel off a frozen speech. If you do, the employer is likely to receive it as coldly as it is delivered.

High-School Graduate— No Previous Experience

If you are a high-school graduate who cannot go on to a residence college but must seek immediate employment, you are badly in need of a job-finding plan. You have to compete, not only with the experienced job-seeker, but with the vast army of other high-school graduates who have just as much to offer as you.

You must recognize the fact that employers generally regard a high-school education as a minimum requirement. However, do not let this cause you to belittle the value of your high-school training. That training is basic training. Without it you will be lost in the shuffle. It has taught you to read, write, and talk intelligently. It has taught you to reason, and without it you could not hope to assimilate higher training or get very far in the business or industrial world.

155

Your first problem, however, is to rise above the high-school graduate competition. That is an easy problem to solve. If you are not sure of the line of work you want to follow, and many young men and women are not, make a temporary decision. Do you want to work in an office; in a shop; or, do you want to get into some type of sales work? Once you have decided, immediately enroll either in a night-school class, or in a home-study course for higher training in the field you have just chosen.

What happens when you enroll for training beyond the high-school level? You immediately add to your qualifications; you rise above the high-school competition; you have more to offer, more to build into your sales talk, and you have proof that you are ambitious—an important factor!

Your job doesn't end there, however. You must now plan a sales talk, and follow the same job-finding campaign as I have outlined in this chapter (see pages 131–151) for experienced job-seekers.

In planning your sales talk, since you have had no previous experience, you will very naturally emphasize the subjects in your high-school course that will be helpful to you in the type of work that you seek. English, Mathematics, etc., will help you materially in office and sales work. Mathematics, Physics, and so on, will help you in shop work. Any vocational courses such as Machine or Auto Shop should of course be mentioned if you are applying for such work. It may even be that your instructor will give you a reference. Add to these facts the subjects in the advanced training course you have enrolled for and you will find that you have material for an effective sales talk.

With these facts you can build a sales talk that will probably induce an employer to give you a chance even though you have had no previous experience. However, if an employer says, *"I am sorry, but we want someone with experience,"* don't stop there. Make your reply something like this:

"I appreciate the fact that it costs money to train employees, but let me go over my qualifications again. I am sure that with the minimum supervision I could work into the position quickly. Your company is the kind of firm I would like to work for permanently, and with my previous training, and the training I am now enrolled for, I really believe I could make good on the job."

A good salesman never takes the first "No" for an answer—that is when he really starts to sell. You can do the same thing, and your chances of clinching a job depend largely on how well you prepare your sales campaign *in advance.*

Conduct at the Time of the Interview

It is probably unnecessary to tell you that the most important thing to do before you leave home to call on an employer is to check on your personal appearance.

Did you bathe? Is your hair neatly combed? Are your teeth brushed? Is your breath sweet? Are your fingernails clean? Are your shoes shined? Are your clothes neatly pressed? These may seem like rather personal questions, but you must remember that employers are—and have a right to be—extremely critical. If you are slovenly in appearance, they have good reason to believe that you will be slovenly in your work.

Bad breath and perspiration odors are touchy subjects, yet they are vital to the discussion. It is hardly possible to be too cautious in this regard as there is nothing quite so disgusting as to talk with a person whose breath is offensive or who exudes an odor of perspiration. You may be sure that such a person is not likely to be considered for the kind of position to which you aspire.

EMPLOYER FIRST: A man should always remove his hat upon entering an employer's office. If the employer is busy, stand quietly in front of his desk until he addresses you. Do not be the first to speak. If you break in on him before he indicates that he is ready to listen to you, you will probably put him in a bad frame of mind.

SHAKING HANDS: Do not offer to shake hands with the employer. If he offers to shake hands with you, shake his hand firmly, but without a display of force.

SITTING DOWN: Do not sit down unless you are invited to do so. The employer may want the interview to terminate quickly, and it is always best to be agreeable to his wishes.

BE NATURAL: When addressing an employer, be natural. Say "Yes, Sir" and "No, Sir." Do not put up a false front. Just be yourself.

SPEAK UP: No employer likes an employee or prospective employee to be timid in his approach.

SIT UP: If you are invited to sit down, do not slouch in your chair. Pull in your stomach muscles, sit straight but not stiffly, and look the employer in the eye when talking to him.

DON'T LINGER: When the employer indicates in one of many possible ways that the interview is at an end, don't linger.

DON'T BEG: Never try to work on an employer's sympathy to secure employment. You may "unsell" yourself very quickly by so doing. Always retain your dignity, keeping your troubles to yourself.

158

Don't Chew Gum or Smoke when talking to an employer.

If you are told that there is no job open but that you will be kept in mind, say: "Thank you. I hope you will consider my application seriously as I really would like to work for your firm." (Rise and leave.)

TESTS

Many concerns use various types of tests to determine your general or specific fitness for a given character of work. These tests are of three kinds:

First: The I.Q. (Intelligence Quotient) Test. Its purpose is to obtain a rating of your native intelligence.

Second: The Performance Test. Its purpose is to determine your speed and accuracy for specific classes of work such as typing, shorthand, etc.

Third: The Aptitude Test. Its purpose is to discover, if possible, abilities and disabilities that will enable the employer to determine in some degree your suitability (aptitude) for a definite type of work.

A great deal could be written on these tests but providing a proper attitude toward them seems far more important than theoretical discussion of their merits. If your mental attitude is right, you need not fear the tests an employer may give you. They are not given to stump you or to put you "on the spot." Their purpose is to supplement other information the employer has about you, and you benefit as much as he does when these methods are employed.

You will agree, no doubt, that the results of the tests are as important to the applicant as to the employer. No one wants to be a misfit because the misfit gains as little as does the employer when this regrettable situation exists.

Tests offer another important opportunity that is often overlooked. They give you a real chance to prove your ability. Here is what Mrs. Rheua Pearce, of the Personnel Department of Marshall Field & Company, Chicago, says:

> Performance and aptitude tests should be welcomed by the prospective employee, especially those who do not possess that sparkling personality that makes an immediate impression on an employer. Such tests give all applicants an equal chance, since the applicant is then judged not on looks or first impressions but on ability.

Welcome any intelligence or aptitude test an employer may give you—don't fear it or allow yourself to become anxiously nervous when taking it. Look at the test as an opportunity to prove your ability. Approach it calmly, do your best, and if you are fitted for the work you are seeking the test will help you to land the job.

CHANGING JOBS

The time may come when you feel you have reached the limit of possibilities in the company you are working for, or that you are in the wrong type

of work and want to make a change. If this is the case, don't act too hastily. Be sure first that you have given enough consideration to the matter. Don't make the mistake of thinking the pastures are greener in the fields beyond your own. Check up with your employer; let him know the kind of work you want to do. Do this tactfully, of course—don't demand a change. If after thinking it over carefully you are still convinced it would be best to make a change, follow these rules:

First: Keep your decision to yourself; don't discuss it with fellow employees, or even with friends.

Second: Don't give up your job; hold on to it.

Third: While you are still employed, put the letter plan outlined in this chapter into operation, as if you were unemployed. Make a list of firms you think might offer you the opportunity you desire and send letters to these companies as directed in the plan.

Fourth: When you get a reply asking you to present yourself for an interview, ask your present employer for time off to keep the appointment.

Fifth: Be sure when you do have an opportunity to make a change that the new position will provide the type of work you wish to do.

Note: Don't get into the habit of changing jobs simply because you can get other jobs. Remember, one of the strongest points in your favor is that you are a steady, dependable worker. Too many changes of position in a short period of time is a mark against you, *not* a recommendation.

Summary of "How to Find a Job"

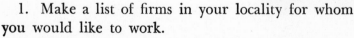

1. Make a list of firms in your locality for whom you would like to work.

2. Look up important facts about these firms.

3. Plan carefully your letters of application.

4. Mail your letters to these firms.

5. To the firms that don't reply to your first letter mail a follow-up letter 30 days after the mailing date of the first letter.

6. If you don't land a job on your first try, add more names to your list and keep the plan working for you. Adverse business conditions in your locality will affect the situation, but don't let that discourage you. Keep right on writing.

7. Before presenting yourself, get all the information you can on the firms that agree to grant you an interview.

8. Prepare the data of your application for employment beforehand.

9. Organize and rehearse your sales talk in advance.

10. Before you call on the employer, check up carefully on your personal appearance and during the interview keep in mind the points of conduct detailed for your guidance.

Compare the methods suggested in this chapter with the haphazard methods many people use when seeking employment, and you will quickly realize why they get results.

PART IV

Getting Ahead

No one but myself can be blamed for my fall.
NAPOLEON BONAPARTE 1769–1821

Let's Analyze the Topnotcher

HAVE YOU a real topnotcher among your business acquaintances? Are you one? Well, perhaps I shouldn't ask that question before we have a chance to find out what a topnotcher is.

Let's Analyze Him

Several years ago there came to my desk a very clever article put out by the magazine *Motor West*. I repeat it here because, in my opinion, the man who could meet the qualifications stated would be a topnotcher in any business organization. The article is in the form of a HELP WANTED advertisement. (See next page.)

Help Wanted

1 A man or woman for hard work and rapid promotion, who can find things to be done without the help of a manager and assistants.

2 A person who gets to work on time in the morning and does not imperil the lives of others in an attempt to be the first out of the office or shop at night.

3 A person who listens carefully when spoken to and asks only enough questions to insure accuracy in carrying out instructions.

4 A person who moves quickly and makes as little noise as possible about it.

5 A person who looks you straight in the eye and tells the truth every time.

6 A person who does not pity himself for having to dig in and hustle.

7 A person who is cheerful, courteous to everyone, and determined to make good.

If interested, apply any hour, anywhere, any place, to anyone.—MOTOR WEST.

He Went Broke

We were discussing differences in people one day not long ago when a friend spoke up and said, "I remember well the first time I went into business. That was back in my twenties, when I thought I knew all there was to know about business and people. When I started out to build a sales agency to sell a newly invented can opener I was positive I'd make a million dollars. Six months later I was stone broke and much wiser for the experience. I had hired just about anybody who answered my ads. It never occurred to me that there was a marked difference in people and the way they worked. I poured out my savings every week in salaries and sales promotion.

"As I look back on that experience I marvel at the fact that I was able to stay in business as long as I did— there was not one topnotcher connected with my first business venture, including myself."

To succeed, every business must have a goodly share of topnotchers on its payrolls. The larger the number, the more successful the business. These individuals are the "spark plugs" that keep the business going through thick and thin. They are the pace-setters and eventually they reach the top jobs.

A Self-Starter

Let's look at the Help Wanted ad again and, as an experiment, let's assume we are in business for ourselves and are faced with the task of hiring people to work for us.

The first paragraph of the ad reads as follows:

A man or woman for hard work and rapid promotion, who can find things to be done without the help of a manager and assistants.

If you had invested your own personal savings in a business it is certain that in order to safeguard that money you'd want a person with ambition—a self-starter who, after having been trained in what to do, would go ahead and do it right without taking up your time in demanding help and direction.

There's an old saying, "The less supervision a man requires, the more he's worth." It's a grand and glorious feeling to have folks associated with you who know what they are doing and go ahead and do it right.

168

Dependability

The next thing you would want would be the kind of person described in paragraph two of the ad.

A person who gets to work on time in the morning and does not imperil the lives of others in an attempt to be first out of the office or shop at night.

Dependability and interest, that's the real "meat" of the above paragraph. First, you would want the kind of person who was interested enough in his job to show up for work every day. Then, too, you very naturally would want him to get to work on time. Why? What difference do a few minutes make? You can answer that question by asking yourself: "What would happen if everybody where I work would start from five to thirty minutes late every day?" If there were enough people involved, the company might eventually go broke through increased costs and delayed production. If that fact is true, then, certainly what is fair for one is fair for all. The people who come late establish a bad practice and are no more entitled to those extra minutes (whether they are paid for them or not) than are all the other employees. You've got to have regulations in every business. If you don't have them, or if they are repeatedly ignored, everybody suffers. The person who objects to regulations in business would yell his head off if, through some co-worker's failure to observe regulations, he would be prevented from earning a bonus he otherwise might have received. Whenever you doubt the value of any regulation in business, study it well. Think of it from the management side before you condemn it or object to it. If it means a saving to the firm, then be FOR it, not AGAINST it, since your own pay check is involved.

Clock-Watchers

The last part of paragraph two has to do with "clock-watchers."

A topnotcher is never a clock-watcher. Usually the person who constantly watches the clock is an individual who is not vitally interested in what he is doing.

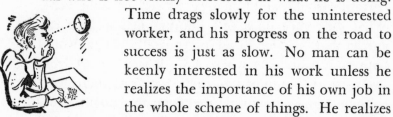 Time drags slowly for the uninterested worker, and his progress on the road to success is just as slow. No man can be keenly interested in his work unless he realizes the importance of his own job in the whole scheme of things. He realizes that every business is made up of a number of jobs and that the efficiency of the organization depends upon how well each individual job is done. Therefore, a topnotcher seldom watches the clock. He is interested in getting his job done in the very best way he knows how. He's the kind of a person you'd like to have working for you if you were in business.

170

Wide-awake

That's the meat of paragraph three:

A person who listens carefully when spoken to, and asks only enough questions to insure accuracy in carrying out instructions.

Have you ever worked with a person to whom you had to give the same simple instructions over and over again? Exasperating, isn't it? Usually this is due to a lack of interest. That lack of interest can be traced to a lot of causes. Many times it is traceable to bad after-work habits.

A topnotcher, the kind of a person you would like to have working for you, prizes health more than a good time. He realizes that deadheads, sore heads, and "bellyachers" are usually suffering from overeating, lack of oxygen, or loss of sleep. The person who aspires to be a topnotcher must beware of any habits that keep him out late at night. The most miserable hours a person can spend at work are those in which he must fight both a headache and the desire to go to sleep. Success will surely pass up those who are listless, sleepy, or ailing. To be a topnotcher, you've got to be in topnotch condition.

171

Quiet Efficiency

The greatest of all "pests" in business are the loud-mouthed, blustering individuals who can't seem to remember that those around them have a job to do and do not like to be interrupted unnecessarily. Then, too, there's the type of worker who, because of lack of planning or lack of interest, makes the simplest task seem difficult and involved. It is very annoying to have to  depend upon this sort of person. They are always behind in their work, and many times they hold up the production of others. You know the type — they muddle around all day picking up things and putting them down. Their desks, counters, or machines are in wild disorder. Toward the end of the day they rush around trying to make up for the time they mismanaged all day long. They waste "great gobs" of energy starting and stopping and jumping from one thing to another.

The type of a worker you would like to have work for you is the kind of a person described in paragraph four of the ad—he's a topnotcher.

A person who moves quickly and makes as little noise as possible about it.

The skillful worker always does his work in the easiest and shortest way. He wastes neither words nor motions—he always plans his work and then works the plan. He appreciates the fact that no one is born with skill; everything that the human being is able to do

172

has to be learned, and skill is the result of long hours of practice, stern discipline, and continual search for better ways of doing things. A job that someone else might handle four or five times before completing it, he handles once. Work seems to pour from his desk or machine in a steady, dependable flow.

In a Mail Order House

Not long ago in a large mail order house customers and the company's salesmen alike started complaining about not being able to get a reasonably prompt reply to their mail inquiries. A general investigation was made and the result was revealing. The investigation was started among the correspondents—the folks who dictate the letters. There it was found that some correspondents dictated two or three times more letters daily than did others. Naturally, the ones making the study were interested in finding out the "why" of this great difference in production. They watched one person whose production was very low and here is what they found. The individual was about as fast as the others when he dictated, but he lacked system and consistency in handling the mail. He picked up a letter, read it, looked around, put the letter to one side, and picked up another, and then got up from his desk to get something or other. When he returned to his desk he started rearranging his pile of mail, looking through his letters until he found a short one to answer. Time and time again he would repeat the process, wasting his time in reading and re-reading a letter instead of picking up the speaking tube of his dictaphone and answering the letter after the first reading. When this fellow's stack of mail was looked over, letters that should have been answered days before were found on the bottom of the pile. When asked about those old letters he said, "I've got to get some more dope on them first."

The next study was made in the transcribing department. There, as well, they found both efficient and  very inefficient workers and a lot of old mail dictated but not typed. Letters that were dictated one day by certain dictators were typed the same day. Letters dictated a week previously were still untouched. Why? Well, here's what they found. Some of the girls worked constantly. Others jumped up and down, doing about everything else but typing. Then, too, it was discovered that some girls liked to do the work of one dictator but not the work of some other and, because of lack of proper super‑ vision on the part of the department manager and lack of teamwork on the part of the typists, customers were badly treated.

It never occurred to the ones who were guilty of delaying the answering of important mail that they were jeopardizing the incomes of every person working for that company, including their own. Their trouble was not necessarily insincerity. They had never learned to work skillfully. It was also discovered that the poor producers were more tired at the end of the day than the quietly efficient workers. Brain fag is often the result of a disorganized plan of action.

174

Yes, we would pick the quiet, efficient worker every time—he's worth his weight in gold.

Reliability

How about paragraph five in the ad?

A person who looks you straight in the eye and tells the truth every time.

We all like the fellow we can depend upon. The most exasperating person to work with is the liar. He's a "No. 1 question mark in business." Give me a man who will look a person straight in the eye and give a straightforward answer. You'll never find him trying to blame others for his own mistakes. If he makes a mistake he admits it and takes the blame unflinchingly. You never find him in "gossip cliques." If he says he'll do something, he does it. If he owes you money, he pays on time. He's the kind of a man you can trust with uncounted money. He's the kind of a person you could put in charge of your business if you were away—he's downright dependable. Dependability is one of the true characteristics of a top-notcher.

Self-Pity

Yes, we're still discussing the kind of a person you would like to have working for you if you went into business, and we are down to paragraph six:

A person who does not pity himself for having to dig in and hustle.

The Complainer

Did you ever work with the type of person who is forever complaining? If you have, you know how irritating they are. They wear themselves out with self-pity. In offices, they keep a constant brew of complaints stirring—the window is open too wide, or not wide enough, this or that is not to their liking. In shops, they complain about regulations, supervision, too much work, or not enough work. They scream to high heaven when now and then an emergency comes

along requiring them to work overtime or do extra work. They seldom stop to think that the extra job to be done may mean the success or failure of the company they work for, thus affecting their own pay checks.

It's not very pleasant working side by side with a person who is so enveloped in self-pity that he makes those around him uncomfortable. Sometimes the chronic complainer turns into a dangerous individual

176

when he reaches the point of knocking the company
he works for. All who listen to his disloyal harangues
wonder how long he will continue undiscovered by his
employers—a dissenter in the ranks, a "drag" in every
sense of the word.

There is a printed sign under the glass on a manager's desk in the lobby of a Texas hotel that reads
something like this:

TO OUR EMPLOYEES

*Our combined job is to make our guests com-
fortable. We must all be one in our endeavor.
If, as part of our working team, you do not
feel you are one of us, if you don't like us,
if you prefer to knock us rather than boost
us, then, for heaven's sake, quit and work
somewhere else before we all lose our shirts.*

That notice contains a lot of good common sense.
It's the kind of a notice (with the first line deleted)
that could be posted on the walls of every shop, office,
or store in the nation. It applies to all workers from
the company president down in every firm that wants
to stay in business and prosper. A topnotch business
must, of necessity, be made up of topnotchers. And
topnotchers are men and women who are builders, not
wreckers.

Elbert Hubbard Said—

Elbert Hubbard, the sage of East Aurora, New York, once said: "A topnotcher is simply an individual who works for that institution of which he is a part and not against it." That's good common sense, too.

Yes, a topnotcher is invariably a booster. The company's interests are his interests; and he never detaches himself from the concern either by word or action.

He may have grievances now and then, but he knows there is a proper place to "air grievances" and a sensible way to settle them without jeopardizing his own and his fellow workers' security by attacking the source of that security.

One thing a topnotcher remembers is that when we compliment our company we compliment ourselves. Listeners think well of the man who praises the services and the products of his company and the company itself. Disparaging remarks made about the company cast suspicion on the individual's loyalty and suggest that he may be a chronic knocker and would probably be the "meat axe" no matter what company he might be connected with. Actually he is looked upon as a dangerous individual. He is like a sailor who scuttles his ship.

178

Cheerfulness and Courtesy

Now we come to the final paragraph in the **ad.**

A person who is cheerful, courteous to everyone, and determined to make good.

A friend of mine was telling me recently about one of the kindest and most lovable characters he ever met— a Pete Evans. He was one of those fellows who wears a perpetual smile. It never made any difference whether it was hot or cold, or cloudy or bright—Pete always wore a smile. It wasn't a stage smile, either. It was a genuinely friendly, cheerful smile—one that made people like to be near him. Once a fellow worker asked Pete where he got that smile. Pete replied, "Well, son, I make it a point to 'wake up' with it every morning and it seems to stick by me all day." Every person in the plant liked Pete. He radiated sunshine wherever he went. In all the years that Pete was on  the job he was never known to say an unkind word to or about anyone. Pete's philosophy was simple. He put it this way: "You can't think or say mean or discourteous things about other folks if you have a smile on your face that starts in your heart."

The day that Pete retired as general superintendent at the age of 69 everybody chipped in to buy him a token of esteem. The day after the presentation the plant was a gloomy place—everybody missed Pete and his sunny smile.

Yes, cheerfulness goes hand in hand with courtesy. One of the definitions given for courtesy in the dictionary is, "An expression of respect." Our friend Pete evidently knew the meaning of the word. He started out as a punch press operator. He resigned as plant superintendent. He commanded not only the respect but the loyalty of others by respecting the feelings of his fellow workers. When someone made a mistake or got behind in his work Pete would "invite," not "order," the man into his office. He'd invariably start off with, "Hello, Joe, how are the wife and youngsters?" Later on, Pete would bring up the matter in mind and talk things over with him in a friendly, courteous way. When a man came away from one of those sessions he wore a smile—Pete saw to that. Moreover, the man did better work from then on and proved himself worthy of Pete's confidence.

Once in a while a newcomer would misunderstand Pete's big smile and get the idea that Pete's plant was a good place for horseplay and practical jokes. It was interesting to hear how Pete handled this type of worker. Without raising his voice, he'd say: "Young fella, you're new here, and we like you but, understand, we just can't allow horseplay or practical jokes in this plant. In the first place, there's too much dangerous machinery around here for horseplay. We wouldn't want you to get hurt, and I'm sure you don't want any of the other boys to get hurt; besides, in practical jokes somebody is always the goat and it just isn't courteous to hurt another fella's feelings, not even in fun." Then Pete would pat him on the back, ask about his folks, and walk away.

Let's analyze Pete's technique. First, he used good psychology, although he would have called it simply common sense. Second, when he had made his point, he didn't keep on nagging, but immediately tried to make the young fellow feel comfortable again—he let him save his face.

Pete $\mathcal{H}$ad a $\mathcal{F}$oreman

Pete had a foreman working under him—a very capable chap so far as his knowledge of machinery was concerned but a man who didn't seem to have any understanding of men. One day this foreman "bawled out" a shop worker in front of a group of men. When Pete got wind of what had happened he had a session with the foreman. "George," he said, "how would you like it if I did that to you?" George immediately began a tirade, telling Pete what a poor worker the man was. When George was all through, Pete said, "How did the fellow feel when you got through with him? I'll bet he was as sore as a boil and as stubborn as a mule. That being the case, you've done the company more harm than good. That fellow won't be worth his salt until he cools down and forgets your lack of decency and courtesy. You'd better call him over and make him your friend again or we'll have to get another foreman. You see, George,  those boys out there are working *with* you and me and the rest of the company. They are not working *for* us. They are a part of our team; they are human beings, and they expect to be treated like human beings. Now, go ahead, George. Go out there and make that fellow feel like he's one of us again."

If you and I had our way we'd like to work with folks like Pete. That being the case, let's be like him. No matter what our job may be we can make it a lot more pleasant if the folks around us really like and respect us. We can do just that if we invariably treat others courteously. After all, no matter what we are doing or whom we are working for, we are part of a team.

Elbert Hubbard summed up the idea when he said: "Civilization is a way of doing things. Civilization turns on organization, and every man's success is a matter of rendering service to others.

"The savage succeeds by looking after Number One. He grabs, appropriates, and fights for the particular thing that he wants. If he succeeds in getting away without being killed he calls it 'Success.'

"No man is ever fired from a firm. He fires himself when he no longer serves that institution. So, in one sense, every man is an instrument of civilization. He is one of the tools with which the Deity works."

And we add to Elbert Hubbard's quotation this last thought—the Deity works wonders with the topnotcher —the kind of a person you would like to have working for you if you were in business for yourself.

The big problem of business today is to get hold of men who will stand the gaff of leadership. It's strange that there are so few.

OWEN D. YOUNG

Satisfaction

IF DAY AFTER DAY you were to ask the average man on the street what gave him the greatest satisfaction in living, you would receive many varied and interesting answers. The answers would embrace all fields of human endeavor from sport to religion. It might surprise you how many times the doing of something — work — is mentioned as the No. 1 satisfaction.

In the beginning, work was supposed to be a curse but it has turned out to be the greatest blessing that ever came to man. Thomas Carlyle, the great Scottish philosopher, once said, "Blessed is the man who has found his work. Let him ask no other blessedness."

Millions of people will testify to the soundness of this simple truth. When a person has found the job he likes and has put his heart and soul into it and gained skill in performance, work becomes the No. 1 satisfaction in life. From the very beginning of life itself, man has been forced to work in order to secure food, shelter and clothing. And through man's determined struggle to improve the quality of his living came all the arts and sciences of modern civilization.

Work itself offers different kinds and degrees of satisfaction. There is the satisfaction that comes from skill, doing something skillfully. There is the satisfaction that comes from doing work speedily. There is the satisfaction that comes from ability to create or invent something.

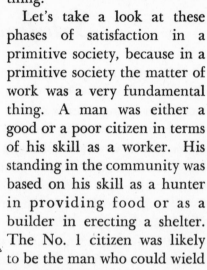

Let's take a look at these phases of satisfaction in a primitive society, because in a primitive society the matter of work was a very fundamental thing. A man was either a good or a poor citizen in terms of his skill as a worker. His standing in the community was based on his skill as a hunter in providing food or as a builder in erecting a shelter. The No. 1 citizen was likely to be the man who could wield a club or shoot farthest and straightest with his bow and arrow, or the man who improved the method of lashing a stone to a limb to make a tool such as a hammer or axe. The top man was the tool user, the man who could use his primitive tools skillfully. And his satisfaction came in the amount and quality of the food he was able to secure for himself and his family, or from his share in serving the community needs—building and defending men against enemies or beasts.

The primitive man soon learned that as he gained skill he also gained in speed of production, because speed results from working with good tools and following good methods. Good methods of doing work are always the easiest and generally the quickest, so skill and speed went hand in hand. Because a man was a tool-using animal he was continually thinking about the improvement of the primitive tool — the piece of stone fastened to a strip of wood. I wonder if you can think a little about what went through the mind of the primitive who was

the first man to sand a wedge, the tool that enabled him to split things with less effort, or devise the lever, which enabled him to move loads. The implements were no more than a pole and a rock, but with the aid of these simple things he was able to move cumbersome loads alone which otherwise would have required the strength of many men.

Then came the roller. He discovered one day that it was easier to roll things than to drag them across the ground. From the roller it was a step to the wheel, and when man invented the wheel he had progressed a long way toward civilization, for the wheel, the wedge, and the lever have not only lessened the burden of man but are, in part, the bases of our

modern methods of production.

There were also the little things—the knife, the sharp edge that would cut a lot of different kinds of material. There was the needle by which one could sew; there was the fishhook with which one could catch fish; there was the arrowhead that made the killing of game easier. There was the bow itself which went through many stages of improvement. It is interesting to note that out of this workaday life of the primitive man, in which activities concerned with securing food, shelter, and clothing were the center of his existence, there grew language, music, pageant, and ceremony. So we come back to Carlyle's statement and see the truth of "Blessed is the man who has found his work. Let him ask no other blessedness."

Today it is harder to see this thing we call work in  its true significance because it has become so complicated. All life is complicated. The efforts and results of a man's work do not stand out now in the way that primitive man's did. They are tied together with the work of everyone else. There are millions of other interests besides the primary one of securing food, shelter, and clothing, and yet work, a man's job, still remains the center of his interest. If we examine it closely we find that in his job a man still lives and moves and has his being. In it the joys and sorrows of his family abide. It is the source of all happiness for himself and his family. It is still the source of his food, shelter, and clothing.

You've heard the story of the philosopher who was passing by the stone quarry and stopped to watch the men at work. He very quickly noted that there were three kinds of workers: The drones who hammered listlessly, the group that just hammered away monotonously, and those who seemed inspired. His inquisitiveness got the better of him, so he walked into the office and told the man in charge of his observation and asked permission to go out in the quarry and ask a few questions of the men. Permission was readily granted.

Walking up to a member of the drone group he asked, "Do you mind if I ask what you are doing?"

"I'm cutting stone," the man replied disinterestedly. "What do you think I'm doing?" . . . "What's the stone for? I don't know and, what's more, I don't care. I'm just a stonecutter."

Going over to the next man, who appeared to be less indifferent than the first, the philosopher asked the same question. The man replied, "I'm carving a pillar." . . . "What's it for? How do I know? They give me the specifications and I do the cutting—that's all."

Then picking out one of the men who seemed to be working with genuine interest he put the question once more. The man stood up proudly. "I'm helping to build a temple that is under construction in Evanston, Illinois. Look at this stone I'm working on. It's the 'keystone' for the archway.  There's a sketch of the completed temple on the east wall in the office. Take a look at it—it's beautiful."

Whether you know it or not, you are building a temple, too, and so are the people who are working with you.

Pity the man who will add to the story of the temple the cynical note: "I'm helping to build a temple for someone else to profit by." In such a frame of mind he robs himself of all the satisfaction an individual should and can get out of his work. His lot is an unhappy one indeed, for if we are to enjoy life we must get our greatest joy out of our work.

Obviously, the stonecutter who felt that he was helping to build the temple was getting greater satisfaction out of his job than the other two men. He was getting a bigger "kick" out of life, too. Let's see if that makes sense. We spend most of our life at our work. If our work is interesting, time passes by pleasantly. We enjoy those hours, and we enjoy coming to work.

The idea of becoming keenly interested in your job and the company you are working for is just good plain common sense. The most miserable person we know of is the clock-watcher. Every day he or she goes through the agony of waiting for quitting time. Yes, time drags slowly for the disinterested worker, and his

 or her progress on the road to success or security is just as slow. The individual who works only for a pay check and quitting time leads a miserably shallow life regardless of what he may do after working hours.

There's a whale of a lot of difference between just cutting stone and hewing out the "keystone" of a temple. One man sees before him an inert mass of stone. The other man sees the temple. Why is it that you can pass down the aisles of almost

any factory or office today and find these same three classes of workers. One lathe operator is striving for perfection, the others are just watching their machines. To the man striving for perfection, the piece of steel in the lathe is something alive. He knows metallurgy. He knows that the bar is made of atoms forming a definite pattern. He knows that it will react in certain ways to certain treatments. His work is seldom found on the scrap heap.

This man not only knows the structure of the metal he is shaping, but he knows, as well, where the piece will fit into the completed article. He is master of his lathe. He realizes its limitations and its possibilities. He is a skilled mechanic. Time passes quickly for this type of worker—he's a topnotcher in his line. His type is not only found in the shop but in offices and behind counters, too.

The top-notch bookkeeper takes real pride in his immaculate and correct set of books. The stenographer is proud of the typed page that looks like perfection; the shipping clerk takes pride in clearing all shipments every day; the advertising man gets real satisfaction from copy that pulls; the salesman gets real satisfaction out of breaking sales records; the correspondent gets a big thrill out of a letter that spurs the reader to prompt action; the supervisor derives real satisfaction out of increased production through skilled leadership. So it goes through each department.

In each case you will find this skilled worker moving forward wherever he is, reaping not only personal satisfaction, but promotions and salary increases as well.

Speed

If you cannot win, make the one ahead break the record.—*Anonymous*

Thus far we have talked about the satisfaction of skill—that expertness of hand and mind which brings all who achieve it success. We are, however, aware that there is another form of job satisfaction, **speed.**

Speed is a real job satisfaction. It is a part of our natural make-up to try to break records. Take the fellow who has knocked a few seconds off a record in a foot race or the one who has stepped up the production of newspapers coming off the press or set a factory record for the number of parts welded in a day. In every case, the worker who made the record increased tremendously his own self-respect and, in addition, earned the respect of his fellow workers. How do these peo-

ple get to be record-breakers? They studied the job and got to thinking about motions, or techniques, that would make the work easier. Making work easier usually results from cutting out the useless motions, or in some cases useless words, the ones that are unessential—in a manner of speaking, it's a sort of cutting across lots to save time. Sometimes a little thing like sitting rather than standing, or the better arrangement of work. In any of these cases there is a scientific approach to the job and, after all, the scientific approach is just finding out the easiest and best way to do a job. The champion typists or punch press operators are those who have eliminated all useless motions, who have put rhythm into their work and cut out clumsy, wasteful motions. The fast workers always show rhythm in the things they do. It's a beautiful sight to see a fast worker in operation, no matter whether it is driving rivets, running a punch press, or a typewriter. We can't all be skilled operators, but we can all get satisfaction in doing our job more efficiently, in turning out more piece parts, selling more goods, writing more letters, etc. Try it. Note the personal satisfaction you get out of setting the pace for others.

Creativeness or Invention

Have you ever thought of how much creativeness and real brain energy went into the invention of the lever by the primitive man? Just think what happened on the day this primitive man discovered that with the aid of a limb of a tree and a stone he could move weights that before he could not even budge.

Think again of the saving of human effort when some primitive invented the wedge that enabled him to split logs with comparative ease, and another invented the wheel that enabled him to move tremendously heavy loads with comparative ease. The engineering sciences were born out of this deep human desire to make work easier and to add to the conveniences and pleasures of living.

When thinking of inventive genius, we naturally bring to mind such names as Edison, Bell, the Wright Brothers, Kettering, etc. These are the "big guns," but did you ever stop to think of the thousands of "little fellows" who are making valuable contributions to the improving of the quality and quantity of production of goods for our use?

American genius in production engineering—the

skills in inventing tools, machines, assembly lines, and organization has made our country the foremost workshop of the world and, by and large, the greatest gains have been made through the thousands of contributions of the little fellows. Thousands of American factories have "suggestion boxes" for ideas regarding the improvement of production, and thousands of ordinary working men have shown marvelous creative ability in being able to improve the shape of a tool or a holding device or innumerable other small devices for speeding up production. And apart from the many rewards that such improvements have brought their inventors the greatest satisfaction has come from the joy of creating. This ability to create is not a native ability. It is possible in every one of us, and, if we stop to think of it, most people can point to some little thing which they invented or created which enabled them to do some part of their work a little better or a little faster. This joy of creativeness or inventiveness is not confined to the working hours of a man's experience. Many of the great inventions and ideas have come out of the avocational interests of people, the hobbies with which they have occupied themselves in the hours after work. And, in these activities they experienced full freedom in playing with new things.

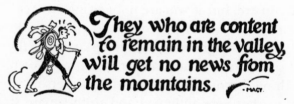

They who are content to remain in the valley will get no news from the mountains. —MACY

Creativeness is by no means confined to things strictly mechanical. A great advertising slogan may take form in the mind of one of the fellows in the production department. A new packaging idea may come from the shipping clerk. A time-saving or money-saving idea may be submitted by a man on the sales force. Each, in turn, gets his ideas as a result of reflecting about things—taking a keen interest, not only in his own job but in bigger things the company attempts. Keep your mind active through trying to create new things, new ways of doing some things better or easier, and taste the everlasting joy which comes from this fruitful experience. The rewards of creating come high—high in esteem of fellow workers—high in terms of gainful reward—and high in self-satisfaction.

The happiest people are those who are conscious of making contributions to their profession, trade or field of endeavor.

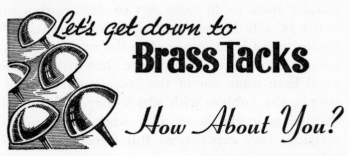

Let's get down to
Brass Tacks
How About You?

Are you getting a "kick" out of your job? I sincerely hope you are, but if you are not getting any real "work satisfaction" I heartily recommend that you do something about it right now—not necessarily for the benefit of someone else but primarily for your own. The first thing I would recommend to a person who has come to that very unhappy and unfortunate stage in life where work has become a necessity rather than a pleasure is that the person ask himself or herself this question:

"What kind of company would my company be if every person employed there were just like me?"

That question makes a person sort of sit back and reflect a bit.

Reflection is the first step to solving the problem of disinterest. There are many more questions to ask yourself after you have answered that first one frankly.

I think the next thing I would do would be to learn more about the company I work for—its products or the service it renders. Maybe you think you already know all there is to know and maybe you are right. Let's see.

Take Some Mental Snapshots

Who started the company? When did it start? How did it start?

What about the product or service it renders? Do you know all about it?

What is the company's competition?

Are you working at top efficiency to help your co-workers meet this competition? You should, your pay check is dependent upon meeting that competition.

What about your job? How important is it?

If you delay in your work, does it delay others?

If you are careless in your work, what happens?

Do you meet the public? If so, do you reflect credit to your company in every contact?

Have you studied your job thoroughly? Each operation or job function?

Have you ever done any outside studying to see how others do the same work?

Are you developing the skill of getting along with your fellow workers? This is of vital importance to job satisfaction.

Would greater skill or speed, or creative ability on your part lower costs, improve the product, or the service, its sale, or increase production?

That last question is most important. Upon your ability to contribute to the success of your company through skill, speed, or creative ability rests your possibility for real satisfaction, promotions, pay increases and security. Of these four true work satisfaction is the greatest and most lasting reward—the other three are the logical results of the first.

Horse Sense and Promotions

AT SOME TIME in your career you may be inclined to say to yourself, "Why should I worry about promotions? I haven't had a promotion in an age. I'm stuck here on one job and don't see any chance of promotion in this company." Maybe you'll be right, but I doubt it. If you are right, what are you going to do about it? If you pull up stakes and quit the job you have, you will probably soon find yourself  in exactly the same fix in some other company, only your chances for advancement will be slimmer, since long service is at least one point in a person's favor in getting a promotion.

No! I can't agree with a person who believes that though he has not made progress in one company he will get ahead in another. That's like thinking the grass is greener in the other fellow's yard.

If you ever get the feeling that you ought to be promoted, ask yourself these simple questions:

199

 Do you know to what job you want to be promoted?

 Do you merit a promotion on the basis of past accomplishments?

 Have you done any outside study on your own time to qualify you thoroughly for the job you want?

 If the job you want entails the supervision of others, are you the kind of person you would like to work for?

Unless you can definitely answer all of these questions in the affirmative, DON'T ASK FOR A PROMOTION; you are not ready for it. Instead, start immediately on a well-planned program of self-improvement, the goal of which will be to enable you to answer YES on every one of the questions.

Money Is Not the First Consideration

Let's see what question No. 1 involves. "Do you know to what job you want to be promoted?" Offhand, that might not be an easy question to answer, but if you are going to ask for a better job you would do well to have a definite job in mind. However, the mere picking of a job that pays more money is not the solution to the problem. There are some more questions to ask yourself. First, are you sure you would like the new job? Second, are you certain it is the type of work that you have a real aptitude for? Wishing for a better job simply because it pays more money is "silly wishing." The salary involved should never (yes, I said "never") be the only reason for wanting to be promoted. An additional amount added to each pay check will never make up for the discomfort of having to work on a job which makes you unhappy or which you are not fully qualified to hold. Yes, the first thing to do is to decide what kind of job you want without allowing the money angle to be the controlling factor.

Check Up on Yourself

Now we come to question No. 2. "Do you merit a promotion?" This question is not quite as simple as it sounds. To get the real answer you are going to have to ask yourself a lot more questions—very searching questions. Since you are conducting this self-quiz you can afford to be brutally frank.

A. Is My Firm Completely Satisfied with the Way I Am Doing My Present Work?

If there is any doubt in your mind about the answer to this question, you are not ready to ask for a promotion. The safest thing for you to do is to improve to a point where there is no question about your ability. The fact that a person has been on one job a long time or wants a change is not a very strong selling point—in fact, it's a very weak one. If you base your request for a promotion on either one of these two points, you may get a change of work but not a promotion.

B. Am I Absolutely Reliable?

A promotion usually carries with it increased responsibility, and the matter of reliability is an important one. How about you? Do you get to work on time? Do you show up for work every day? If you say you are going to do something, do you always keep your word or do you sometimes substitute an excuse for performance? How about the payment of bills? Do you have an excellent credit record? Remember, a business firm has no reason to believe that an employee will handle its business well if the employee displays a lack of ability to handle his own affairs properly. If you haven't developed a reputation for absolute reliability, start now—before you go after that better job or the chances are you will be turned down.

C. Do I Cooperate?

Be very frank with yourself on this point. If you haven't been as cooperative with your fellow workers as you should be, start now and develop a reputation for cooperation—before you ask for a promotion.

Dust Off the Slate

Question No. 3 of this quiz involves the matter of preparation by study. "Have you done any outside study on your own time to thoroughly qualify for the job you want?" If you can't answer YES to this question, get busy now! Start on a study program that will fully qualify you to hold the job you think you want. Go about this quietly.

Don't Broadcast Your Plans

Keep your study plans within the confines of your family circle. You can easily see why you should do this. If you let it be known generally that you are studying to get some definite job, your efforts may be misunderstood by your fellow workers. Some people will even go so far as to try and see that you never reach your goal if they get the idea that you are out to get somebody else's job. Yes, keep your plans to yourself.

Another good reason for keeping your plans to yourself is the fact that you may find, by studying in the new field, that you do not like that kind of work after all. Or you may discover that you are not cut out for that type of work. If you make such a discovery through study at home, your time has been well spent and you still have an unhampered chance to select some other type of work as your ultimate goal. It's

204

just as valuable to know what you can't do as it is to know what you can do, providing you make that discovery yourself and in the privacy of your own home.

Do People Like You?

Now, let's look at question No. 4. "If the job you want entails the supervision of others, are you the kind of person you would like to work for?" Here we consider a very important point—our ability to get along with other people. Do people like you? Be honest about it. If they do, fine! However, if you can count a number of people you work with who don't like you, then you have a job to do before you even think about asking for a promotion.

Many otherwise capable individuals are not promoted to positions of responsibility simply because they cannot get along with their fellow workers. If you were the manager of a firm, you would not put a person in a position of responsibility if that person was heartily disliked by his fellow workers, would you? Of course not. That being the case, it is only horse sense to make sure that you are liked and respected by the people you work with. There is no reason to believe that the individual who cannot get along with people in one department can get along with the people in some other department.

Chase the Jinx

In a previous chat we discussed in detail some of the things that cause us to lose the respect of others and to lose friends. Let's look at them briefly. We called them Tongue Boners. Here they are:

1. Sarcastic remarks about fellow workers
2. Gossiping about fellow workers
3. Running to the boss with complaints about fellow workers
4. Losing our tempers

Take a good look at yourself. Have you been guilty of any of these tongue boners? If so, now's the time to stop making them and set about making people really like and respect you. Do that before you ask for a promotion or you may never get a chance to demonstrate your ability to hold a better job. This discussion is getting mighty close to a talk on person-ality so let's see if we can define the word. What is your definition of personality? Do all people have it, or is it something only a chosen few possess? The answer is that we all have a personality—some good, some not so good, and some bad. Fortunately, it is not a difficult matter to improve our personality to the point where people will like us. One of the simplest rules is to make sure that we always treat others as we ourselves would like to be treated. We don't like to be spoken to in a sarcastic manner; we don't like to have others gossip about us behind our backs; we very definitely do not like to have others run to the boss and make complaints about us; nor do we ever want to bear the brunt of someone else's fit of temper. These facts should keep us from making enemies.

Every Friend Is a Lucky Horseshoe

It is impossible for me to emphasize too strongly the necessity of constantly keeping after the job of making friends. Every friend is a lucky horseshoe. Without friends a new job—a promotion—is a risk rather than a thing to be desired.

At a club meeting of sales executives not long ago a Mr. Coates, internationally known sales engineer and lecturer, gave a rule for making people like to work with you. Mr. Coates said: "Treat every fellow worker as if he were a customer you would like to sell a bill of goods to."

No one likes to work with surly, cross, and irritable people, and, above all, no one likes to work under their supervision. Don't bring a sour face to work—start the day with a smile.

All right, we've discussed the four questions we are to answer before asking for a promotion. If you feel you pass the self-examination with a grade of 100%, then there is one more thing to do: sit down and write out in detail your qualifications for the job you want. Are these convincing to you? If not, they won't be convincing to anyone else. If you are satisfied on this point, then make your next move—talk the matter over with your foreman, manager, or supervisor. Sell that individual first; you need his full support—get it, and you will in all probability eventually get the job you want.

One More Important "Don't"

If you apply for a promotion and the promotion is not immediately granted, DON'T LOSE YOUR TEMPER. Smile and ask that you be considered for the next opening. Remember that you have had a chance to present your qualifications for a better job—and this is an opportunity in itself. As a result, you will probably be considered for the next promotion that comes up.

A Truism

 Usually the people who yell the loudest about being held down or underpaid are the ones who have never done one single solitary thing on their own to merit any more than they are getting.

*The habit of going to the bottom of things
usually lands a man on top.*

The Next Rung on the Ladder

THE AMBITIOUS PERSON is always looking forward to the time when he can take the next step up the ladder. Yet, very few people realize that a promotion is a definite turning point in their careers. The way an individual acts during the first few weeks on a new job may either hinder his progress in an organization or open the door to opportunities which mean further advancement. Therefore, when we advance another rung on the ladder, we should give serious consideration to the fact of promotion—regard it earnestly.

Promotions generally come to people in one of the following ways: (1) Through demonstrated ability on a former job; (2) by virtue of term of service, putting them next in line; or (3) because of having done something outstanding on their own initiative.

An Important Event in Our Careers

There are other reasons, but regardless of what may have been the reason for a promotion, the first thing to remember is that until a person actually makes good on the new job he is on probation. The length of the period of probation depends upon the individual—not on someone else. If he allows the promotion to go to his head, if he criticizes the way the job was done previously, or if by overconfidence he dashes into the new work ignoring instructions or refusing to listen to others, thereby making a lot of mistakes or a lot of enemies, his term of probation will probably be short and he will have good reason to be sorry promotion came his way.

Yes, a promotion is very definitely a turning point in a person's career. If he makes good, he "continues on up the ladder." If he fails, advancement with the company may be blocked for a long time to come, perhaps for good.

212

When Opportunity Knocks, Be Humble

One of the first rules to observe when promotion comes your way is to be humble. Remember, you are on trial not only with the management but with your fellow workers, your immediate superiors, the person at the next desk or machine, the group you sit at table with—in fact, with everyone connected with the company.

The braggart loses friends faster than he can possibly make them. If a person feels like blowing off steam because of a promotion, then let him do it, *but* do it where no one else can hear him, preferably in front of a mirror where he will soon discover how silly bragging is.

There are several reasons why we must say to ourselves "Be humble" when fortune smiles upon us in the form of a promotion, and here is the most valid of them all. By the manner in which we accept a promotion, our fellow workers are either for us or against us. They may all be envious—there's no harm in that—but are they glad we were promoted or do they think the management made a great mistake in giving us the promotion? You may say: "I don't care what they think." You do care, however, for no one can succeed unsupported.

When you were a youngster, did your parents at some time or other move from one town or neighbor-hood to another, making it necessary for you to "break in" with a new group of playmates? Well, if you have ever gone through the experience of being the "new kid" in the neighborhood you know that youngsters can be downright cruel or wonderfully helpful and friendly. To a certain degree, you are a newcomer when you take over a new job, and the people closely associated with you can be just as cruel, or helpful, or friendly as the youngsters of your childhood days.

ℋe Knew ℋow

The surest way to get the friendship and help of your co-workers is to ask their help. That's what we mean by being humble. At lunch not long ago a businessman was heard to say: "Of all the men I've worked with, one man stands out in my mind. I still remember his name, although I haven't seen or heard of the man for over thirty years. When we first met I was a file clerk—he was the new sales director. I was making $7.00 a week—his salary was in the hundreds a week. The second day on his new assignment he walked up to my files and, after introducing himself, he said: 'Will you help me? I'm a newcomer, and I just won't know where to find what I want. I'll be very grateful if you can show me what I am to do when I need certain records.' "

No Wonder He Was "Tops"

"From that day on I worked my fingers to the bone for that man. It didn't occur to me then, but I know now why he was one of the highest paid men in the industry. He was humble in spite of his outstanding ability and high position, and through his own humility he caused everyone associated with him to like him, deeply respect him, and work their hardest for him."

We may not all reach a place in life where we can command such a salary as did that sales director, but we'll come a lot closer to increasing our incomes by having others help us along the way than by trying to do it alone. The fact is that one never gets very far as a "lone wolf."

Since it is undeniable that to succeed we need the help and support of others, we should always seek it in a friendly way.

A Few Important "Don'ts"

There are some very important "Don'ts" to remember in getting adjusted on a new job. Here are a few:

1. Don't stick out your chest. Keep it where it belongs. In the words of St. Paul, a man should not "think of himself more highly than he ought to think." It's natural for you to feel a little "set up" about being promoted, but that doesn't mean that you are the special gift of Heaven to the organization. If it so happens that you are smarter than those around you, it will show in good time.

2. Don't pretend to know more about your job than the person who is assigned to teach it to you. If you refuse instruction, or receive it with a know-it-all air, you can be fairly sure your instructor will tell you only the minimum of what you ought to know. He will be inclined to leave out all those little extras which can mean so much to the success of your work. Learn all details that anyone is willing to explain; soon enough you will be expected to know them.

3. Resist the temptation to always "have a better idea" than the one which your instructor is trying to convey to you. You were not hired to make over the company but to get out work. Later on, when you get your bearings and are accepted as a "regular" there

216

will be time enough to make tactful suggestions regarding changes to those responsible for operations and procedures. For the present you don't have enough information to make your suggestions carry weight. So save your breath—and the temper of others.

Be Grateful

4. Be grateful for the help you get on the job and show that you are grateful by the way you speak and act to the people who help you. Nobody can "go it alone" in business; if he tries it he will be left alone— and out in the cold to boot, in a very literal sense.

5. Don't promise more than you can perform in a specified time. If you repeatedly promise to do something in a stated period and later have to apologize for failure to deliver, you will shake everyone's confidence in you. This is another instance where it is important not to think of yourself more highly than you ought to think.

6. Show an interest in helping other people with their work if you are asked to do so. You will very likely learn little things which you could learn in no other way; you will widen your circle of acquaintance and show the kind of spirit which your equals and superiors in the organization will appreciate.

What About Supervision?

Most promotions carry with them responsibility for the work of others. This responsibility is a heavy one whether it involves the supervision of one or many. To be placed in charge of the work of others is a real challenge to the worth of the individual. It no longer is a question of *How good a worker is he?* Instead, it becomes one of *How good a boss will he make?*

To some individuals authority is like wine—it goes to their heads and can wreck their careers. At the beginning of this article it is suggested that we should regard promotion objectively—give it earnest thought.

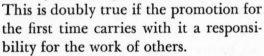

This is doubly true if the promotion for the first time carries with it a responsibility for the work of others.

Of necessity, during the war emergency, many men were promoted to supervisory jobs which they were totally unqualified to hold. They were skilled in their trades but totally unskilled in getting along with other people. They yelled at men, they threatened, they had favorites and prejudices, and in one way or another these things hindered production. Many of these men learned the hard way that there is a right and wrong way to handle people and get work done quickly and efficiently, and that way is through development of teamwork.

At an executive conference a company president was heard to say: "I can't understand why our employees are not more loyal. We've given them bonuses, insurance policies, hospitalization, and everything else we can afford and still they are not loyal." The vice president spoke up and said, "But, John, you can't buy loyalty. You've got to earn it. All the things we have done are fine and, in a way, they are appreciated, but we must make our supervisory staff understand

218

that they must get our people to work with the company instead of for it, or our efforts to promote loyalty will fail." That vice president was right. The trouble wasn't all with the workers—it was to some extent the fault of the supervision they were receiving.

Successful Supervision

The most successful supervisor or executive is one who can get people to work *with* him and the company rather than *for* him as a boss. Harmony, efficiency, and productivity all come as a result of teamwork. Teamwork is possible only when there is loyalty to a purpose. Loyalty can only be earned—it cannot be bought or forced.

A Lot of "Don'ts"

There are a number of rules for the development of skill in the handling of human beings. Here are a few:

219

1. Use the word "we," not the word "I." ("Let's go" is a lot better slogan than "Get going.")

2. Stay pleasant, no matter how tough the pressure may be. (A smile is contagious and people work better wearing a smile rather than a frown.)

3. You can "bawl out" a mule but not a human being. Don't lose your temper and, by all means, don't make the mistake of correcting people in the presence of others.

4. If a person needs correcting, start with a smile. Use reasoning and understanding. These will go a lot farther than arguments and harsh words, and when you get through you will have a friend—not an enemy.

5. Boost the people under you. Pass the credit on down to them. Don't try to "hog it" yourself. Their success will be a direct reflection of your efficiency and capability for supervision.

6. Don't take sides in an argument between members of your working team. A suspicion of favoritism will kill teamwork. Get all the facts before drawing a conclusion.

7. Don't spread gossip or listen to it, and don't encourage horseplay.

8. Show a sympathetic interest in the other fellow's troubles, but don't discuss your own.

9. Talk all you want about the company, its staff, its policies and other departments, but be sure that every word is *for* and not *against*. You cannot expect loyalty from others if you are not 100 per cent loyal yourself. If you have any complaints, take them up with those over you and don't "air" them before those from whom you expect to get teamwork.

10. Be extremely tolerant, especially in giving in-

structions to others. The thing that seems very simple to you may seem very complicated to someone else. Time invested in giving instructions clearly is a mighty profitable investment.

Yes, there are a lot more rules, but the sincere application of these ten suggestions will go a long way to make you the kind of a person with whom you yourself would like to work.

This chat contains a lot of "don'ts" but they are the kind that are well worth reading many times over. A promotion is a very important turning point in our lives. We fight hard for a better job—for the next rung on the ladder. The most pitiable person to behold is the person who is demoted because he could not measure up to the responsibilities that a promotion carried with it, or one who allows promotion to go to his head. When  promotion comes your way, pitch in and make good, but don't trample on the people under you. They are the ones who can either pull you down or push you farther up the ladder.